Diary
of a
Blind Magician

Secrets of the Amazing Haundini

Gary Haun

Illustrations by William Haun

authorHOUSE®

AuthorHouse™
1663 Liberty Drive
Bloomington, IN 47403
www.authorhouse.com
Phone: 1-800-839-8640

First published by AuthorHouse   9/03/2010

ISBN: 978-1-4490-8253-6 (sc)
ISBN: 978-1-4490-8255-0 (e)

Library of Congress Control Number: 2010904672
Cover photo by Roger Kyler
Cover design by William Haun and Chris Sisson

Attention: Some of the tricks in this book require the use of small objects such as coins, safety pins, paper clips, etc. These objects can be a choking hazard to a child. It is recommended that the tricks be performed by adults or with adult supervision. Under no circumstances should a child be allowed contact with any small object that may be a choking hazard.

Printed in the United States of America
Bloomington, Indiana

This book is printed on acid-free paper.

Dedication

This book is dedicated to Renee. She is more than a great magician's assistant. She is more than the wind beneath my wings. She is the real magic in my life.

Contents

Introduction

The world of magic has brought me in contact with many amazing people. I first met Gary Haun at a magician's convention in Las Vegas. He was interested in my Project Magic, in which magic is used in hospitals as physical therapy and to help in the rehabilitation process. Gary told me that my work had inspired him to become a magician and that he would now like to use magic to help others.

I was indeed glad to have Gary involved in Project Magic. You see, Gary is blind. After that meeting with Gary, I found out that he was an accomplished stage magician. He has since performed magic for thousands of people. However, I think Gary's real magic is in the way he connects with people. He has shown others how to overcome their limitations and how to deal with adversity—especially those with disabilities.

Gary has become an inspiration to many. The amazing thing about Gary is not that he is a blind magician but how he has used magic to help overcome blindness.

In this book you will find more than some good magic. You will read how Gary has used magic to light up the world for himself and others. While you will learn to do some excellent magic, you will also learn how Gary had to adapt magic so he could perform it.

I am honored to know Gary as a fellow magician and a person who has brought real magic into the lives of others.

—**David Copperfield**

David Copperfield is the most successful magician in history. He is not only an inspiration to magicians but an inspiration to all who aspire to be the best they possibly can be. With the encouragement of such a great magician as David Copperfield, I don't feel like a "blind magician." I feel like a magician who is doing the best show that he can with the ability he has.

Welcome!

Welcome to the world of magic! I hope this book helps you to get started in learning the art of magic. The tricks you are about to learn will be fun. They are not complicated and do not require any expensive props. After mastering a few of these easy to do miracles, you will be able to astonish others!

Take your time in learning these effects (tricks). Practice them until you are very confident in your handling and presentation. Some of the tricks presented in this book are classics of magic. Some of these effects are used by professional magicians. With that in mind, you have an opportunity to carry on a part of magic history.

I am just as excited today about learning a new magic trick as I was when I first started over thirty years ago. I want to share this excitement and enthusiasm with you. No matter what age you are, you can enjoy learning to do magic. Attitude is everything! The more you learn, the more confident you will become in performing a magic routine.

I also have provided you with some other information about magic and some resources that will help you in your pursuit of learning magic. Congratulations on taking the first step to a fun and entertaining way of learning the art of conjuring. Whether your dream is to become a professional magician or just to learn a few entertaining card tricks, you have come to the right place.

The real magic in life is in never losing your interest in learning something new.

The Amazing Haundini

The Amazing HAUNDINI

"Adversity has the effect of eliciting talents,
which in prosperous circumstances would have been dormant."
—Horace (65–8 BC)

My interest in magic began at an early age. When I was six years old, I read a book about Houdini. Little did I know at that time that one day I would be doing some of the same tricks and stunts that he performed.

During that same time period, I recall watching magic performed live and right before me. James Leonard was not only my uncle but quite an entertainer. He was talented in many areas but the one that I remember most is his expertise at thimble magic. He could make a thimble appear and disappear "magically" and had a routine in which the thimble would disappear, penetrate a hat, and then reappear inside the hat. Of course, I know how this is done now, but at six years old I thought it was real magic. My uncle didn't just do a magic trick. He presented it as a funny story. And therein lies the secret of real magic. It is not in the trick itself—it is in the presentation of the trick.

I also remember my first magic show. I attended Whig Hill Elementary School in Rockford, Illinois. The school seemed more like a huge family than a school. The teachers were very caring and kind. My classmates were friendly, and it seemed we all cared for one another. A school assembly was a big event. There were many, but the one I remember most was the magic show.

I do not remember the magician's name, but he was very entertaining. He wore a tuxedo and held a black wand with a white tip. He *looked* like a magician. The first thing he did was to hold up a single piece of paper that had a huge dot on it. He immediately turned the paper around and showed two dots on the other side. When he turned the paper back to the other side, it now had two dots on it where there originally had been one! He then turned the paper around again to the other side—and it now had three dots! Eventually, he turned the paper around to reveal it now had six dots on it! It was amazing. I now do this trick (called Dots Impossible) in my kids magic show.

The magician performed many wonderful and entertaining tricks that day, like the Comedy Funnel and the Candy Factory. In the Comedy Funnel routine, the magician appears to pour water from the elbow of a kid in the audience. It was very funny. In the Candy Factory routine, the magician showed a glass filled with sugar and in an instant, he turned the sugar into several pieces of hard candy.

The trick I enjoyed most, however, came at the end of the show. The magician blew up a balloon and placed it on a tray. He tapped the tray with his magic wand, the balloon popped, and in its place was a beautiful white dove!

During the late 1950's and through the 1960's, I would occasionally watch magicians on TV. There was Mark Wilson with *The Magic Land of Allakazam*, which was shown on Saturday mornings. I also recall many famous magicians who appeared on the variety shows, such as the *Ed Sullivan Show*.

During my junior high school years, I took dramatics and was involved in almost all the school theatrical productions. I know now that this was important in my eventual decision to become a magician. The school shows gave me knowledge about stage movement, stage presence and, most of all, confidence before an audience.

In 1970 I joined the United States Marine Corps. I talk about my experiences in the Marines in my first book, *Vision From the Heart*. I can honestly say that everything I have needed to survive in life was taught to me in the Marine Corps. I have faced every challenge in my life with the skills the Corps taught me. It is indeed true when you hear someone say, "Once a Marine, Always a Marine."

I was in a helicopter squadron, and I made it to the rank of sergeant. I loved being a Marine, and with the exception of the birth of my son, being a Marine was the proudest time of my life. I liked my fellow Marines, and it really was like a family. I knew I could count on my fellow Marines, and they knew they could count on me.

One day in 1973 I was asked to run a hydraulics test on a helicopter. As a hydraulics technician, I had done this task several times without any problems. However, this day would be different. I had just gotten the test stand to full pressure when I noticed a leak coming from the front of the test stand. I went to check it out and as I leaned over it, the hose exploded.

I don't remember much from that day. I suppose I have repressed most of it. What I do recall is being in the naval hospital, where a Navy doctor told me that I was permanently blind in both eyes. I was twenty-one years old. Many things went through my mind at that time. At that time I thought my life was over, but I wasn't ready to give up. Life is tough sometimes. I have always said that attitude is everything, and I decided that I would fall back on the philosophy of the Marine Corps: "Adapt and Overcome." And that's what I did.

At that time, magic seemed very far out of my life. Like many things in life, however, the magic found me. When I was in the Hines Veterans Hospital for Blind Rehabilitation Training, I met another blind veteran named Jerry Miller. He had another name—a stage name: "Mr. Impossible." As strange as it sounds, I was introduced to magic by a blind magician!

Jerry performed stage and close-up magic. One of the tricks he did was the classic Scotch & Soda. In this coin trick, a Mexican centavo is magically changed into a quarter. In honor of Jerry, this is the first trick I do in my close-up magic routine. Jerry would often talk about different magic tricks and how he performed them. It was at the hospital that I decided that I would like to become a magician.

After I left the hospital, I sought out a magic dealer. I found out about a local magic shop called Magic Manor. I went to the store, introduced myself to the owner, Rich Gough, and told him that I would like to get started in magic. He was very enthusiastic and very helpful. Never at any time did he suggest that my being blind would be a problem. At first he recommended self-working tricks that could be done without complicated moves. The beauty of these tricks was that I did not need eyesight to perform them. The tricks also helped my self-confidence for doing magic.

Rich is not only a very good magician, but he also is very knowledgeable in all areas of magic. His real strength, though, is in teaching magic. It takes a lot of patience to teach magic. Many difficult sleight-of-hand techniques require an enormous amount of repetition in the learning process. Rich developed certain methods and techniques just for me because of my lack of eyesight.

Eventually, I took close-up magic classes and learned many of the classic close-up magic tricks. I then put together a close-up magic routine. I have added to it in the thirty years I have been doing magic, but I still include many of the tricks that I was originally taught. For example, I still do Scotch & Soda, Three Card Monte, MacDonald's Aces, Matrix, and a Sponge Ball routine.

After I became comfortable performing close-up magic, I made the move into stage magic. Once again, I started with self-working props and other apparatus that was not too complicated to perform. I eventually mastered enough effects to put together a small stage show.

I started performing in nursery schools and nursing homes. This was a great place for me to gain confidence in my presentation. In my kids show, I would use effects like the Magic Coloring Book, Hippity-Hop Rabbits, the Egg Bag, and the Clatterbox. The Clatterbox is a wooden box that falls apart when a spectator tries to open it as the magician has.

In my nursing home show, I would do more tricks with music. I would do the classic silk routines, such as Twentieth Century Silks, and Blendo. Blendo is a silk routine in which four silks magically change into one multicolored silk.

Once I became confident in my performance with these types of audiences, I learned to do illusions. I would perform the Sword Box Illusion, Zig Zag Lady, the French Guillotine, and the Sword Through the Neck. The Zig Zag Lady is an illusion in which my assistant is divided into three sections with two large metal blades. I then push the middle section out and away from the other two sections. The illusion is a modern day version of the Sawing a Lady in Half trick, only now it is enhanced by pushing out the middle section.

My next step in magic was to learn to work with doves. I must say this remains one of my favorite routines. Doves are beautiful, and the audience really seems to appreciate my producing a dove. I do many different dove effects. A few of my favorites are the Dove Pan, the Dove Bag, and Silk to Dove. These are all different ways to produce a dove.

Over my thirty years in magic, I have performed for just about all types of audiences. I have done school shows and corporate parties. I have performed for over a thousand people in an outdoor theater, and I even performed a trick while skydiving and while scuba diving with sharks! I did a *quick* coin production and vanish while I was on a tandem skydiving jump in 1994. I also did a coin trick for the divemaster while I was shark diving in the Bahamas. (I have a picture of the sharks that surrounded me on the cover of my first book, *Vision From the Heart.*)

I have met many famous people through magic. I met Muhammad Ali at a magicians convention in Las Vegas. He really enjoys magic and was interested in the type of magic I did for children in hospitals. He frequently visits hospitals and said he likes doing magic for the kids he meets.

I also met my close and personal friend, Dr. Jane Goodall, through magic. I first performed close-up magic for her at one of the Jane Goodall Institute's Roots & Shoots summits. Roots & Shoots is a fantastic program for young people that emphasizes conservation and preservation of animals, caring for our environment, and concern for each other. The program stresses that one person can make a difference.

I have performed magic at other JGI summits also. One of my favorites was one that was held at the Biosphere II near Tucson, Arizona. Another favorite was the College Summit held in Fort Worth, Texas. The people who attend these summits are so much fun and such a great audience. They are enthusiastic about magic and energetic about doing something positive for the planet.

I have performed magic in many different countries around the world. While I was in Africa, I performed magic in some interesting places. I did a close-up routine in Hermanus, South Africa, and later that same day, I did a kids show in Gansbaii, South Africa. This is significant because the next day, I went to dive with the Great White Sharks. What an awesome experience!

In January 2000, I was asked to appear on the *Rosie O'Donnell Show*, where I performed two tricks for Rosie and her audience. Performing before a live television audience is usually reserved for the top magicians in the country. I was honored to have been given the opportunity.

In 2009 I was asked to perform magic for a full-length theatrical film, *Jane's Journey* (2010), which is about the life of Dr. Jane Goodall. "Dr. Jane" often speaks about me in her lectures. I also am listed as one of her *Reasons for Hope* (Warner Books, 2000). A movie crew from Germany filmed me performing magic, doing Japanese swordsmanship, and skydiving. Only a handful of magicians have performed magic both on a live national television show and in a full-length film. I would venture to say, however, that I am the only blind magician in the history of magic to have had the honor of both opportunities.

Along my path to learning magic, I have met many great magicians who have helped me to succeed in magic. One such magician who helped me with many of my routines is Bill "Magic 500" Hunter. Bill is one of the finest "walk-around" magicians in the country. His celebrity status comes from the fact that he has performed at the prestigious Indianapolis 500 Raceway for over forty years. Bill also performs at many corporate functions throughout the year. Bill taught me the Headline Prediction trick that I performed on the *Rosie O'Donnell Show*. Another magician who has been helpful is Mike "Magic Mike" Winters. Mike is a working professional who performs around the country. Like many magicians, Mike studies magic and is quite knowledgeable on technique and presentation. In fact, although he has great sleight-of-hand skill, his real magic is in his presentation. He performs at all levels of magic, from close-up to stage, and his show is very entertaining.

I also have attended many magicians conventions, which have been a great source for learning new tricks and routines. At these conventions, I have received encouragement from many of the greatest magicians in the world. Dai Vernon, Tony Slydini, David Copperfield, Siegfried & Roy, Johnny Thompson, Norm Nielsen, Jeff McBride, Eugene Burger, and Lance Burton all have given me words of encouragement and praise that has helped me to succeed in magic. This was especially helpful when I was just beginning to learn magic.

When I was in Hawaii for a magic convention, I had the opportunity to talk to Harry Blackstone Jr. (1934–1997) in a Baskin-Robbins ice cream store near Waikiki Beach. He told me that he thought it was really great that I was doing magic and that I had a unique opportunity to inspire other people, especially those with disabilities. At a convention in Las Vegas, Dai Vernon, known as the "Professor of Magic" (1894–1992), told me, "Overcoming adversity is *real* magic. Magic is not done with the eyes. It's done from the heart." I took those words to heart, and that has been the real magic of the Amazing Haundini.

The Amazing Haundini performs the Headline Prediction trick for Dr. Jane Goodall. "Dr. Jane" is probably best known for her research of the chimpanzees in Gombe, Tanzania, in Africa. She is also known for her work in animal preservation and conservation, as well as her commitment to protecting the environment.

I met Muhammad Ali at a magicians convention in Las Vegas. He loves magic and especially enjoys doing magic for children in hospitals.

It was a great experience to be on the Rosie O'Donnell Show. *Rosie was in the film* A League of Their Own, *which was about the Rockford Peaches, a team in the All-American Girls Professional Baseball League. As I live in Rockford, I gave Rosie a Rockford Peaches T-shirt that was signed by some of the original Peaches. Rosie loved it. Courtney Cox Arquette, who starred in the TV show* Friends, *was also on the show.*

Bill Hunter is probably known best as Bill "Magic 500" Hunter, as he has performed at the world-famous Indianapolis 500 for over forty years. He has performed magic for such well-known racing greats as Al Unser Sr. and Al Jr., A. J. Foyt, Mario Andretti and many more.

Bill is one of the finest magicians there is and specializes in "walk around close-up magic." Bill is highly sought after for corporate events and other social events. He is a great example of what magic is all about. He has been performing magic for over sixty-five years and is still performing professionally at the age of eighty-six!

Secrets of a Blind Magician

"How can you do a card trick if you can't see the cards?" I suppose I have been asked that question a hundred times. It sometimes seems that the impact of my doing a magic trick has a lot to do with the fact that I am blind—there are not too many blind magicians. I suppose people know that it takes a tremendous amount of time and dedication to learn magic without eyesight. I also am often asked, "How long did it take to learn that?" Good sleight of hand techniques can be complicated, and as a blind magician, I have had to learn patience. I have practiced for many hours to learn close-up and stage magic.

There are basically two categories of blindness. A congenitally blind person is someone who was born blind. An adventitiously blind person is someone who had sight and lost it later in life. At one time I worked with blind children and adults at the Winnebago Center for the Blind. I taught recreational therapy and living skills, as well as exercise classes, self-defense, and many other recreational skills. I observed that some of the congenitally blind people seemed to learn easier and with less frustration. This is because they were more conditioned to their blindness—they'd always learned without sight. A congenitally blind person, however, does not have the concept recognition and perception of someone who was once sighted. For example, I could describe a bowling ball to a blind child, but until he felt and held one, he would not know what I was talking about.

An adventitiously blind person, however, likely would have seen a bowling ball before losing his or her sight and therefore could form a mental picture of a black or multicolored ball with finger holes in it. A negative aspect, though, is relearning how to do simple activities that many sighted people take for granted. In my own experience, something that once was easy to do became frustrating when I lost my sight. Putting toothpaste on my toothbrush or pouring a cup of hot coffee was a real challenge. It would frustrate me that I couldn't read my mail—I had to depend on someone else to do that for me. (Now I have a reading machine that reads all my printed material.) My point is that I had to learn to do things differently.

For someone who is born blind, it might be difficult to appreciate what a magician is doing. While someone may explain the magic act, the congenitally blind person has no point of reference and may not find the magic act as interesting as it would be if he could see it. I can relate in this way: I am a certified scuba diver, but I can't really appreciate the beauty of the ocean when I am diving. I do appreciate the *activity* of diving, though.

I can remember how much I once enjoyed watching a magic show. I also had a mental picture of what a magician did. I had a concept recognition and perception of what I might have to learn if I wanted to become a magician.

The difficulties of a blind person's learning magic can be many, but they are not insurmountable. I knew that I would once again use my Marine Corps training to help me succeed. In combat training, all Marines learn a saying: "Adapt and Overcome". This basically means that you must figure out a way to accomplish the mission. I have used this philosophy to deal with all aspects of my life, but it has been especially useful in learning magic. It was never a matter of whether I could learn magic. It was more of a matter of what I needed to do differently to master the skill.

The first concern of any successful magician is practicing a certain routine. Many sighted magicians practice in front of a mirror to see if they are doing the technique correctly. Others may videotape themselves and then play it back to see it as an audience would see it. As a blind person, I obviously cannot do this. So I went to magic classes at a local magic shop. Then, once I learned how to do a certain trick, I took private lessons so my teacher could watch my technique. The teacher would tell me if I had any "bad angles" or if I was "flashing." Flashing refers to exposing something in a trick that is not supposed to be seen by the audience or in a way that might reveal how the trick is done.

Once I learned a routine, the next step was getting the confidence to do it before an audience. Once again, I feel it helped in this regard that I once had eyesight. I could remember how a magician would move, and this gave me an idea of how I wanted my magic show to look. It helped with stage presence and with my confidence before an audience.

Obviously, my stage presence depends on my knowing where I am on stage. I have to be 100 percent sure of where my props, tables, and curtains are located. This is accomplished by many hours of practice and, of course, having my props and tables in the same spot each time. This is why it is important for my assistant to know exactly where to set the tables and props. I do not want to have to feel around, trying to find something in a routine. This looks very awkward and is distracting for the audience.

A blind magician needs to use some techniques that a sighted magician does not need. For example, in card magic, a sighted magician can "glimpse" a card. Glimpsing is when a magician looks at a card (usually on the bottom of the deck or the bottom of the cut portion) and remembers it so he can use it later in the routine. This is something I cannot do, but I do not get frustrated about this. My philosophy in life is not to worry about what I can't do. I only need to concentrate on what I can do. I have always tried to minimize my weaknesses and maximize my strengths. My secret is in knowing what a card is before a routine, or the spectator needs to (unknowingly) name it for me so I can use it later in the routine.

There are other methods I sometimes use to know what the card is and where it is in the deck. The secret to this is called "marking" or "gaffing" a card. Several techniques are used to mark or gaff a card. A sighted person can mark a card with a written mark—a very small mark that is made with a pencil or pen on the back of the card. This mark is so small that it is only recognizable to the magician. A visible mark would not help me at all, so I use physical marks or gaffs.

Physically marking a card goes back in history to the days of the riverboat gambler and saloon cardsharps. They would use their fingernail or a sharp point on a ring to mark a card while it was in play. They would make a small cut at a certain spot on the card so that they would know the card by feeling it as they dealt it out. In this manner, they would know which cards another player had. This gave the card hustler a tremendous advantage in the game. The mark on a certain card could also be felt while the cardsharp was cutting the cards. This enabled him to cut to a desired card.

The methods I primarily use to mark a card are pegging, crimping, bumping, or indenting. Sometimes I will use a combination of all of these methods. At one time, these methods were closely guarded secrets. While you might use these methods in home card games for fun, they should never be attempted in a casino. Please heed these words of caution: Do not try *any* of these methods in a high-stakes poker game or in a casino. You could get into a lot of trouble. Las Vegas, Atlantic City, and other well-known gambling places are well aware of these methods, and they take a very dim view of marking a card in play. In fact, it is illegal to do so.

I will explain how I use these methods. Pegging is done by pushing your fingernail or a sharp object into the edge of the card. This makes a small cut in the card that you can feel if you slide your finger down the card. It also enables you to feel the card while it is buried in the deck. This gives you the ability to cut to that particular card.

Crimping a card is somewhat like pegging, except the card is not cut. You merely make a crimp on the card with your fingernail or a sharp object. This can give you the same results as pegging, but it is not as permanent as a "peg."

Bumping is a method in which a small bump is made on the card. This is done with a sharp pointed object, like a needle or a safety pin. This "bump" can be placed anywhere on the card. A differently located bump will identify one card from another.

Indenting a card is the process of actually making a small indentation on the edge of the card. The indentation may be round, square, or V-shaped. Certain cards could be marked with a different "indent" so that you know exactly what the card is just by touching it.

On some occasions, I need to know how a deck is "set up"—this refers to the order of the cards. My secret is that I have a reading machine that tells me what a card is. I have a screen-reading program called JAWS (Job Access with Speech) that speaks as I type. In fact, I wrote this book using JAWS. I also use Kurzweil Omni, a print-reading program. It can read just about any printed material. So when I need to know a card, I simply scan it, and then Omni tells me what the card is.

First I determine the order that I want the cards to be in the deck, and then I use a rubber band around the card box to identify the deck as the one I want to use in a particular routine. If I have three different decks for different routines, I will place the rubber bands in a certain order. The first box will have a rubber band at the top of the box, the second box will have a rubber band in the middle, and the third will have a rubber band at the bottom. It is a simple yet effective way for me to keep organized.

When it comes to coin magic, I sometimes need to know which side is heads and which is tails. Usually, I can feel the difference in the sides of a coin. The relief features on a Kennedy half-dollar are easier to detect than the features that are on a dime. When I need to know which side of a coin to show to the audience, I will mark that particular side. I use a small file to make a small mark on the edge of the side that I want to identify. This mark is very small and cannot be easily detected by the audience. It looks very normal, as many coins are worn down from hitting other coins.

As a blind magician, organization of my props is very important. This is why my close-up case is lined with Styrofoam. I have inserts in the Styrofoam for cards, coins, sponges, and other close-up items. This makes it easy for me to locate the props I need for a certain routine.

Stage magic presents its own challenges for a blind magician. I must always be aware of where the audience is and also where my tables and props are. This is important so that I know how to display a prop so that the audience can see it. More important, I need to be aware of the angle that might expose the workings of the trick. I often use tactile identification to detect the location and orientation of a prop. I use a product called Loc-Dots, which are tiny raised dots with an adhesive back that can be placed on just about any surface. I will stick them on a prop so I can arrange the prop correctly. I also use a product called Bump Dots, which are like Loc-Dots, only bigger. I place them on larger props as a way to know which way the prop is facing. Both Loc-Dots and Bump Dots are available in clear plastic, so they cannot be seen by the audience.

Of course, it is very important for me to know where I am located on stage. My secret here is the use of slip-proof tape that I put down on the area of the stage where I will be working. This type of tape is sometimes used on stairs to help prevent people from slipping. It is like a roll of sandpaper with an adhesive backing. I put the tape down in a large configuration of the letter T. The vertical part of the tape helps me to stay orientated to the audience, as it points directly to the center of the audience. I can feel the texture of the tape with my foot and adjust my positioning accordingly. The horizontal part of the tape lets me know how far out I am in front of my tables.

Another question people often ask is: "Have you ever fallen off the stage during a show?" While this is certainly possible, I take precautions to prevent it. For example, I will set up my curtains and tables as far away from the edge of the stage as possible, or I will put a long piece of the slip-proof tape about four feet from the edge of the stage. When I can't use either of these methods for one reason or another, I employ a method that only a blind magician would need to use. I run a length of "invisible" thread across the entire stage! This thread is sometimes called magician's thread. It is very fine and cannot be easily seen by the audience. I run the thread from one side of the stage to the other about waist level. I then can walk out toward the edge of the stage but stop when I feel the thread.

When it comes to learning new magic, I use several different methods. When I hear about a new trick, I will seek another magician for advice on whether it is a trick that I might be able to do. I then seek out someone who has been doing the trick for a while and who is also a good teacher of magic.

I have learned many magic tricks from reading books. If you wonder how I can read a book, the answer is that I can get almost any book on audiocassette or CD, so I can listen to it. If an audiobook is not available, I can send a print copy to Recordings for the Blind, and they will put it on tape for me. (This is the same method I used to get my textbooks for college put on tape. Recordings for the Blind is a wonderful service. They do great work.)

The majority of the time I read by scanning my books with my reading machine, the Kurzweil Omni. I simply scan the printed material, and the computer reads it back to me in synthesized speech. Of course, it can't "read" a picture, drawing, or illustration, but I can usually figure out what to do if the printed instructions are well written.

I would rather not be thought of as a blind magician as much as a magician who just happens to be blind. In most of my magic shows (especially school shows), I prefer that the audience not know I am blind until after the show. I do this for two reasons. First, if the audience knows I am blind, they may watch the show in a different way—they may look for clues that I am blind instead of concentrating on the performance. If I have to reach for a prop and can't find it right away, the audience may feel uncomfortable. If they don't know I am blind, however, they may think it has something to do with misdirection or something to do with the routine. Second, it makes more of an impact to tell the audience after the show that I am blind. I feel there is a greater appreciation then for the time and effort it takes for me to do a good magic show.

In this book I will teach you many of the magic tricks I have learned over the last thirty years. They are easy to learn and require no complicated sleight of hand. Take your time when learning the tricks in this book. I am sure you will find that the time it takes to practice is well worth it when you show the tricks to your audience. Try them on your friends and family first.

Welcome to the world of magic!

The Coin Control Card

The Coin Control Card is one of my favorite methods of locating a card. Because I can't see the cards, it is important for me to know where my "Key Card" is located. I first read about this method in a book titled *The Magic of Matt Schulien* by Philip Willmarth.

I never met Matt Schulien, and I'm sure that he didn't have a blind magician's special needs in mind when he came up with the Coin Control Card, but I am sure I would have liked him. Matt Schulien (1890–1967) owned a restaurant in Chicago called Schulien's, where he would perform magic for his customers. By all accounts, Matt Schulien was one of the nicest persons ever in the history of magic. He created many magic tricks that are still used by magicians today.

There are many fantastic tricks in *The Magic of Matt Schulien*. I highly recommend this book. When I read about the coin card, it seemed like something I could use—and I have been using it for over thirty-five years! I want to thank Matt for this "gift."

The Coin Card is made in a very simple manner. Just place a coin on the center of a card, as shown in the illustration. Any coin will do, but I prefer to use a quarter. Press down around the edges of the coin until there is an impression on the other side of the card. You do not have to press very hard. A slight indentation on the back of the card is all you need (see illustration).

The magic of this card is that it elevates the cards above it. This makes it very easy to cut to this card. All you need to do is gently lift up on the cards. The Coin Control Card makes a natural break—it will be on the top of the bottom portion of the cards. When a chosen card is placed on top of the Coin Control Card, it's possible to reveal it in many different ways. It is also an excellent way to "force" a card. Forcing a card is a method that lets a spectator think he is freely selecting a card, when that card is actually controlled by the magician.

I am sure Matt Schulien did not know it at the time, but he created a blind magician's dream. I am able to perform hundreds of card tricks with this method. Thanks again, Matt.

The Coin Control Card

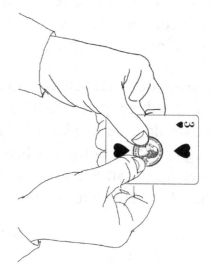

The illustration on the left shows where the coin is placed on the face of the card.

The illustration on the right shows how to push the coin down with your thumbs on the face of the card. At the same time, use your fingers to push on the card from the back. Keep doing this until there is a raised impression of the coin on the back of the card.

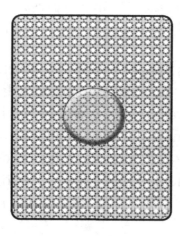

Here is where the raised impression should be on the back of the card. This also shows a view of how the card will appear from the side.

The Magician's Assistant

Not all magicians have assistants. With close-up magic, table-hopping, and manipulation acts, you may not need to use an assistant. However, as a blind magician I feel my stage magic is enhanced by an assistant.

My assistant, Renee, has several responsibilities, including:

- Organizing the magic
- Packing the magic props
- Ensuring the animals are comfortable when transporting them
- Organizing the music
- Setting up the show music, lights, curtains, tables, etc.
- Selecting the volunteers from the audience
- Caring for the animals used in the show
- Transportation
- Record keeping

As a blind magician, it is important that all my props are set in a specific place on the stage or on my table. Renee ensures that each item is where it should be. This eliminates my having to feel around to try to find props, which can make the performance look awkward.

As is the case with all stage performers, a magician's assistant must always be concerned with stage presence and appearance. Many times assistants are used in illusions, such as Sawing a Lady in Half or the classic Sword Box. An assistant is a very important element of presenting a successful magic show.

The Rules of Magic

The following rules are simple but very important if you want to be a successful magician.

Practice often. This is one of the most important rules of magic. Take the time to practice a trick many times before you ever do it for an audience. Practicing will help you with two things. It will help your self-confidence in performing the effect, and it will help you to learn patience. I practice an effect a minimum of four hundred times before I perform it for an audience.

Never reveal how a trick is done. Once the secret of how a trick works is exposed, it loses its entertainment value, as there is no surprise or mystery to the effect. Your job as a magician is to entertain your audience by sharing with them something that is impossible to do or defies belief.

Some magicians expose magic on TV. This is bad for magic because they don't teach you to do magic or tell you how to perform the trick. The sole purpose is to expose the secret of a trick. The illusions exposed on these shows are very expensive, costing thousands (or hundreds of thousands) of dollars. It also takes a lot of time to rehearse the illusion and usually involves using many assistants. Professional magicians earn a living by performing magic they do. If the entertainment value of magic is taken away by exposing the secret, then the ability to perform an exposed trick is also taken away—and this hurts not only well-known magicians but local magicians as well.

Exposing a trick is not the same as teaching a trick. While this book explains how to do the trick, it also tells you how to set it up and perform the trick. It is designed to teach someone who is interested in magic how to do magic. By buying this book you have made an investment in magic, much like taking magic classes. Even if you do not intend to ever perform magic, you will see that it takes time, effort, dedication, preparation, and a devotion to the art of magic to perform it properly.

There are certain methods that I only discuss with other professional magicians. I have certain "secrets" that are closely guarded. Like many magicians, I have several different methods for performing the same trick. The magic I perform in my close-up routine and my stage magic is known only to other magicians. Obviously, if everyone knew how I did everything in magic, I would have no magic to perform.

Remember that exposing the secret takes the "magic" out of magic. The secret of the trick is what provides the mystery that audiences love.

Never repeat a trick. Once you have done a trick for an audience, do not repeat it for the same audience. Doing so will expose how the trick works.

Know what you are going to say. "Patter" is the talk or words magicians use during their act. Not only is it important to practice the technique of an effect, but it is just as important to practice your patter—know what you are going to say as you do the effect. Talk through your practice sessions, just as you would in an actual performance.

Take care of your props. Even if you just have a deck of cards, take care of them. Magic props can be expensive. I suggest keeping them in boxes and wrapped in cloth to keep them from being damaged. Big stage illusions are very expensive and should be handled like a fine piece of furniture.

Study. Read as many magic books as you can. You can obtain many of them from your local library. There are also some very informative magic related websites. Another way to learn magic is to watch videos. There are many DVD's that teach you how to do magic tricks. They usually show how the trick is performed before an audience and then explain how the trick is done. I would also recommend taking magic classes at a local magic shop or from a knowledgeable magician.

Be patient. It might take some time to learn to do a trick the right way, but it will be worth the time and effort you put into it. Don't worry about making mistakes. The more you practice, the more confidence you will have in your routine.

Have fun! You will find that performing magic can be as enjoyable for you as it is for your audience. I try to use as much humor as possible in my magic routines. Once you have mastered a few of the tricks in this book, try them out on your friends and family.

Types of Magic

Within the art of magic there are several categories. Some magicians prefer only card magic, while others perform strictly with coins. There are stage magicians who perform illusions and some who only do close-up magic. Many magicians are proficient with different types of magic. On one occasion they might be performing on stage for a huge audience, and at other times they might be doing close-up magic at a table for a few people. Here is a list of some of the different types of magic.

Bar magic. As the name implies, bar magic is usually done by a bartender who is also a magician or by a magician who performs for bar patrons. Bar magic is usually close-up magic, performed with small items such as cards, coins, sponges, etc.

Bird magic. Many people associate doves with a stage magician, but many different species of birds are used in magic. Parrots, canaries, parakeets, cockatoos, and of course doves are sometimes used in different magic acts. Just about any type of bird can be used in magic in some way. I personally use doves in my stage act. I love working with doves, and there are many different effects in which a dove can be produced or vanished. Some of the best known dove tricks are Silk to Dove, Balloon to Dove, the Dove Bag, and the Dove Pan. In all of these effects, a dove is produced magically.

Bottle magic. In this type of magic, bottles are produced, vanished, and multiplied. One of the classic effects in bottle magic is Topsy Turvy Bottles, in which a spectator tries (but fails) to duplicate the same results as the magician. Multiplying Bottles is an effect in which many bottles are made to appear from one bottle.

Candle magic. In my candle routine I use appearing and disappearing candles made by Fantasio. I end the routine with Multiplying Candles, in which I show one lit candle and then produce three other lit candles from it. Color Changing Candle is a trick in which a candle magically changes color. Some candle tricks are used along with another type of magic. For example, sometimes an Appearing Lit Candle is used to ignite a Dove Pan or Flash Paper. An Appearing Lit Candle is an effect where the magician reaches inside his coat and pulls out a lit candle!

Note: Candle magic usually involves fire and should not be attempted by children or beginner magicians. You should seek instruction from a magic dealer or teacher.

Cane magic. Magic tricks with canes are usually used in a stage performance. Some of the best known cane tricks are Appearing Cane, Disappearing Cane, Color Changing Cane, and the Dancing Cane. The Dancing Cane is an effect in which a magician displays a cane and then makes it levitate in front of him. The magician then "dances" with the cane, making the cane circle around behind him and then twirling it while it is still suspended in midair!

Card magic. Without a doubt, card magic is one of the most popular forms of magic. There are many fine magicians who specialize in performing card magic, and hundreds of different effects can be done with a deck of cards.

Close-up magic. Close-up magic is exactly what the name implies—it is magic that is performed very close to the audience. It is usually done with small items, such as cards, coins, sponges, etc., but almost any small item can be used—pens, salt shakers, paper clips, rubber bands. Advanced close-up magic may involve complicated sleight of hand techniques but it is well worth the time it takes to perform it.

Coin and Money magic. Coins can be made to magically appear or disappear or to change to a different denomination. One of the best known coin effects is Scotch and Soda. In this trick, a centavo is changed into a quarter while it is still in the spectator's hand! Hundreds of different tricks can be done with coins or bills.

Comedy magic. The goal of comedy magic is to perform magic in a way that makes your audience laugh. Many props are available that by their very nature are funny. The Breakaway Wand, for example, is a trick wand that falls apart when handed to a spectator. Several routines use regular magic props but are presented in a comical way. I try to use humor in all of my magic routines, whether it is stage magic, close-up magic, or my kids magic show.

Cruise ship magic. This refers to a location where you perform magic. There seems to be a magician on just about every cruise ship. He usually performs close-up magic at tables as well as performing in the nightly stage shows.

Egg magic. This is a type of manipulative magic. Eggs are magically produced out of thin air and then caused to disappear. Many eggs can be produced from a single egg. One of the best known egg effects is the classic Egg Bag. In this trick, an empty bag is shown, and then a spectator reaches inside the bag to find an egg!

Escapes. This area of magic goes way back in time. Usually, the magician (called an escape artist) is confined in some way. Rope, handcuffs, shackles, and padlocks are used to confine the performer. The magician somehow escapes from his confinement. The legendary magician Houdini was probably best known for his escapes.

Fire magic. Fire magic is an effect that uses fire or some type of flash. Many times a Dove Pan is ignited before the production of a dove. A lit candle can be made to appear from the performer's jacket. Props such as the Hot Book and Hot Wallet erupt in flames when opened. Flash paper is a special type of paper that ignites quickly and burns very fast. It is used in many different types of magic. Note: Fire magic can be very dangerous and should not be attempted by children or those just beginning magic. It is important to seek proper instruction before attempting any effect using fire.

Flower magic. Tricks with flowers are very beautiful and are great for stage magic. I am currently using the Blooming Bouquet in my stage show. I show an empty metal tube and drop a single flower dart down through it. I then raise the tube to show the flower, and then I cover it again with the tube. After a few times of raising the tube, I then lift up the tube to produce a full bouquet of flowers. Other classic flower effects are the production of flowers from a silk and causing a flower to visibly change color. Flower effects can be very expensive but can make a small show look big.

Gospel magic. Gospel magic is usually done within a theme of religion. It is often done in churches or other religious gatherings. Many of the effects used in Gospel magic are standard magic props, but the presentation is religious in nature.

Holiday magic. Holiday magic relates more to when a magic show is performed—it is usually themed around a certain holiday. There are magic shows for Christmas, Halloween, Fourth of July, and just about any other holiday celebration, and magic props are made specifically for holiday shows. For example, the classic Egg Bag is made in the form of a Christmas stocking. Sometimes during a Christmas show, a magician will use a Dove Pan to produce an enormous quantity of candy canes.

Illusions. Illusions are large stage props or apparatus that usually are performed on stage before large audiences. There are hundreds of different types of illusions. Some of the classic illusions are Sawing a Lady in Half, the Sword Box, and Stack of Boxes. In the Stack of Boxes, a magician displays a small box that is only about two feet high. He then stacks a few more boxes on top of the first box, opens the doors on the sides of all the boxes, and out steps his assistant! The Substitution Trunk is another well-known illusion. In this effect, the magician shackles or handcuffs his assistant and places the assistant in a trunk. The trunk is padlocked and sometimes secured with chains. The magician then stands on the trunk and pulls a curtain up over his head. In an instant, the curtain drops, and the assistant is now standing on the trunk, and the magician has vanished. The assistant unlocks the trunk, which is opened to reveal the magician.

Kids show magic. Children's magic is very entertaining and fun. Kids show magic is performed at birthday parties, schools, day-care facilities, or any other occasion that calls for entertaining a group of children.

Liquid magic. As its name suggests, liquid magic uses liquids in a magic trick. The Magic Milk Pitcher is a good example. This effect consists of showing a large pitcher full of milk, which is then poured into a pan. The magician makes a motion as if he is going to throw the pan of milk on the audience, but all that comes out of the pan is confetti. The milk has vanished! There are also tricks in which a bowl of goldfish is magically produced or a glass of liquid is magically changed into a different color.

Livestock magic. All types of livestock have been used in magic shows. Of course, the bunny rabbit is a well-known favorite that is produced by magicians. Magicians have also used dogs, cats, birds, ducks, and many other animals. While exotic animals such as tigers, lions, and elephants are not really considered livestock, they are very much a part of many large stage magic productions.

Manipulation magic. This routine involves many different techniques and movements that are put together for a complete effect. Manipulation can be done with just about any object, but some of the most popular are cards, coins, candles, canes, thimbles, cigarettes, and billiard balls. A performer may produce an item and then make it vanish or change colors. The performer might then produce a large number of the same item or make the object change into a larger or smaller object.

Mentalism. Mentalism is also known as magic of the mind. It usually involves mind reading or prediction routines. A magician who specializes in mentalism is sometimes called a mentalist. Hundreds of effects are made just for mentalism.

Paper magic. This trick uses paper or tissue paper. One of the classics of paper magic is the Torn and Restored Newspaper Trick. In this effect, a magician tears a large section of newspaper into several smaller sections. Magically, he restores the newspaper to its original condition.

Parlor magic. Parlor magic is another name for a small stage show. A living room was once referred to as the parlor. In past eras, people would gather in the parlor to hear someone sing or play a musical instrument. Performing magic in the parlor was a great form of entertainment, and the term stuck. It is a show that is somewhere between close-up magic and a large stage show.

Production magic. The term production magic is applied to any magic trick in which an object is produced. The object produced may be as small as a coin or as large as an elephant.

Restaurant magic. Restaurant magic refers to the venue in which magic is performed. Logically, restaurant magic is done in a restaurant or dining facility. The magician might walk around the tables, performing close-up magic, or he might be sitting at a table in the area where customers wait for a table.

Rope magic. Magicians have been doing rope tricks for many years. One of the most popular rope tricks is called Professor's Nightmare. In this effect, a magician shows three different lengths of rope. One is short, one is medium length, and one is long. Magically, the magician changes all three ropes into the same size. He then restores the rope to the original different sizes. One of my favorite rope tricks is the Sliding Knot Trick. In this effect, a knot is tied on a length of rope. Then the magician asks two spectators to each hold one end of the rope. Magically, the magician slides the knot across the length of the rope.

Silk magic. I love silk magic because it is easy to pack, yet it can be done in a stage show. A silk is a delicate piece of material. Silks come in many different sizes and colors. Silks can be produced by several methods and can be vanished in many different ways. Silks can be used as a cover for a production effect or used to make an object vanish. One of the classics in silk magic is Twentieth Century Silks. In this effect, two silks are tied together and then pulled apart. Magically, a third silk appears, tied between the first two silks. Another popular silk trick is Blendo. This is a trick in which four different silks disappear and are changed into one multicolored silk. Silk tricks are great for those who are just starting to learn magic.

Sponge magic. Many different objects are used in sponge magic. Probably the most widely used are sponge balls. The magician makes the sponge balls appear from nowhere and causes them to magically switch places. Most magicians who perform close-up magic have a sponge-ball routine. The Multiplying Rabbits is also a favorite trick of magicians. In this trick, two sponge "rabbits" magically appear in a spectator's closed hand. The big surprise is at the end of the routine, when the spectator opens their hand to reveal that the two big rabbits have been joined by a handful of baby rabbits.

Stage magic. Stage magic usually refers to a large magic show. It is often performed on stage before a large audience. Most props for stage magic are large so that they can be seen from a distance. Some stage shows require the use of an assistant or volunteers from the audience. Large stage shows may require sound and lighting equipment and backdrop curtains.

Street magic. Street magic has become very popular since magician David Blaine has appeared on television. His TV specials primarily highlight his street magic. It is usually performed on sidewalks or other areas where there is a large gathering of people.

Trade show magic. Trade show magic is done at conventions, corporate events, and trade shows. The purpose of trade show magic is to highlight a company's or corporation's product and to draw interest in whatever the company is selling or to highlight the service that is provided.

Walkaround magic. Walkaround magic is exactly what the name suggests. The magician walks around, performing magic. This type of magic is very popular at large parties, banquets, hospitality rooms, and corporate events.

**A Tribute to
Gizmo, the Magical Rabbit
(1979–1991)**

Many magicians use animals—not only doves and rabbits but all kinds of animals—in their magic shows. The magicians I know treat their animals more like pets than "living props." The audience loves to see an animal in the show. It seems each animal has its own personality.

I'm fond of all animals, whether they have fins, feathers, or fur. As with many pet owners, I become very attached to my pets. In fact, I originally wrote to Dr. Jane Goodall when one of my pets died. Since that time I have become close friends with "Dr. Jane" and like her, I have a deep affection for animals. I have used many different doves and rabbits in my stage show. Each had a different personality and loved the attention that people gave them. While they were all special in their own way, one that I will never forget is Gizmo, the Magical Rabbit.

Gizmo was a Himalayan dwarf rabbit. He was so small when I first got him that he could fit in the palm of my hand. He was very energetic and seemed to be happy all the time—and he brought happiness to me. He was lovable and loved being on stage. He especially liked being held by people, especially children.

Gizmo eventually got so big that he looked like a furry bean-bag chair, and he could no longer fit in the production box that was used to make Gizmo "magically" appear.

I am not afraid to admit that this retired Marine Corps sergeant cried like a baby when Gizmo died. He was my friend. He was always there to bring me up when I was down. I will miss him, and he will not be forgotten.

Magic Tricks for Beginners

The following list of magic tricks are excellent for those who are just getting started in magic. Hundreds of magic tricks are well suited for the beginning magician. This is a small list of some of the tricks for beginners with which I am familiar. They are easy to do and do not require any sleight of hand or fancy manipulation. These are the first tricks I learned when I got started in magic, and I still use some of them in my routine. They are relatively inexpensive and fun to learn. For other easy to do tricks, just ask a magician or contact a magic dealer.

Tree of Diamonds. This is a fun, easy to learn card trick. In this trick, three cards are shown. Two of the cards are face cards (Jack, Queen, or King), and the other card is the Three of Diamonds. The magician turns the cards over and removes the middle card. It is now a TREE of Diamonds with an actual picture of a tree with the diamonds on it.

Shrinking Nickels. This is a minor miracle, in which five nickels change into five really small nickels. This is a good beginner's trick in coin magic.

Nickels to Dimes. This is another fantastic coin trick, in which five nickels change into five dimes. This is easy to do and a great pocket trick.

Coin Vanish Box. A small box with a drawer is used for this trick. A coin is placed in the box, and the drawer is closed. When the box is opened, the coin has disappeared. This is a self-working trick, meaning that the box does the magic for you and it requires no sleight of hand.

21 Cent trick. This trick has been around for a long time. The magician shows 21 cents to the audience. He then places the coins on his palm and closes his hand to make a fist. He removes a nickel from his closed fist and asks a spectator, "How much is left?" The spectator will of course say, "Sixteen cents." The magician then opens his hand to reveal that nothing is left! All the other coins have vanished.

Zig Zag Card. In this trick, a playing card and a frame, which is about twice the size of the card, are shown to the audience. The frame has three small windows (top, middle, and bottom) on the left side, and one middle window on the right side. The magician slides the card into the frame so that it's first revealed in the right side window. He then slides the card over so that it is displayed in the left side three windows. Then he slides the left side middle section of the card to the right side, showing the middle section in the single window, separated from the top and bottom sections on the left side. The magician then slides the middle section back to the left side, and removes the card from the frame, showing it to be just one complete playing card. This is a self-working trick and requires no complicated moves.

Mental Choice. This is a good mental magic effect. I still do this in my close-up routine. The magician removes three cards from an envelope, each with a different colored spot on them. The magician asks a spectator to choose one of the cards. This is a completely free choice. The magician reveals that he had predicted the chosen card.

Dime and Penny. The magician places a penny on the table. He then covers it by placing a small wooden block over it. Magically, the penny turns into a dime.

Ball and Vase. This magic trick goes back to ancient times. The magician shows a small vase with a ball in it. The ball magically travels from the vase to the magician's pocket. He then makes the ball jump from his pocket back into the vase.

Hindu Prayer Vase. The magician shows a small bottle-like vase and a rope. The audience can inspect these. He lowers the rope into the mouth of the vase and, while he is still holding on the end of the rope, turns the vase upside down. He then turns the vase back up and lets go of the vase. Magically, the vase is suspended from the rope. The magician can even swing the vase from side to side with the rope.

Card Magic

Card Magic Made Easy!

Card magic is one of the more popular types of magic. Many magicians, both amateur and professional, do nothing but card magic. One of the many reasons for the popularity of card magic is that it does not require expensive props—you can perform entire routines with just a deck of cards. Card magic is also relatively easy to learn—with some basic instruction, you can perform magic in a short time. Hundreds of card tricks can be mastered by using very easy methods and technique.

I was taught to do card magic in many ways. At first, I was taught basic card magic at a local magic shop. Later, I learned new routines by attending magic lectures. I also studied different card techniques and methods in books and video. The latter was sometimes difficult for me, as I couldn't see the illustrations or pictures, but I had a basic understanding of what the instructions were, and I figured out a way to do the technique.

I learned most of my magic from other magicians, who helped me with handling technique and sleight of hand movements. They would perform a routine and often explain how they did it. I would then adapt the trick so that I could perform it. The tricks in this book are easy to do and require no complicated moves, but once you master these particular tricks, you may want to learn some advanced card magic.

After you practice a trick many times, you'll be ready to show it to your friends or family. Remember to make the routine entertaining by injecting your personality into it. Do not repeat the routine word for word as given in the instructions. Add or remove words to make the presentation comfortable for you and enjoyable for your audience. I try to inject some humor into my close-up card magic as well as my stage routine. The important point is to be relaxed in your presentation, as it helps the audience to feel relaxed.

Follow the instructions in this section on card magic, take your time, and practice the moves until you are very comfortable in your presentation.

I was taught these tricks many years ago, so I have tried to cite the proper sources of the trick. I have researched many books in an effort to find the inventor of the trick or the origin of the trick. (I sincerely apologize if I haven't given credit to the proper creator of a particular trick.) There are many variations on similar types of tricks—some tricks have the same movements but may be called different names. There may be several different ways to achieve the same results of a particular trick. For example, there are over a hundred ways to force a card.

There are also many different ways to locate a chosen card. These are sometimes called Prediction tricks or Card Revelations.

I suggest that you learn a few easy to do tricks at first to become comfortable in presenting them. The audience can lose interest with tricks if the presentation is too lengthy or if the tricks are too complicated and hard to understand. A card routine should have a smooth, relaxed feel for both the magician and the audience.

Card Basics

Basic terms and techniques will help you to understand what needs to be done when performing card tricks. Here are some of the basics.

There are fifty-two cards in a standard deck of cards, each with a back and a face. Here are some examples of different card backs. (See illustrations).

Each deck of cards contains four suits— Diamonds, Spades, Clubs and Hearts. Diamonds and Hearts have red index numbers or letters, and Spades and Clubs have black index numbers and letters—the index indicates the card's suit and its value. For example, a Two of Hearts would have a number 2 and a heart in the corners. This card would also have two hearts on the center of the card—these are called "Pips" or "Spots."

A Number card is sometimes called a "spot card," but in this book, I will refer to the cards with numbers one through ten as "Number cards."

A Face card is sometimes called a "Court card." The Face cards are the cards with faces on them—the Jacks, Queens and Kings.

There are four Aces in a deck of cards, one for each suit—the Ace of Spades, the Ace of Diamonds, the Ace of Clubs, and the Ace of Hearts.

Card Basics

On the left is an illustration of the back of a Bicycle brand Rider-back card. It is poker size. This type of card back is very popular with card magicians.

On the right is an illustration of the back of an Aviator brand card. This is a bridge-sized card—it is not as wide as the poker-sized card.

There are many different card backs. Corporation logos, holiday theme photos, company advertisements, and photos of animals are but a few of the things you might find on the back of a card. I have a deck of cards that have my business card photo on all the backs.

On the left is an example of a Face card. Face cards are also referred to as "Court cards". The Face cards are the Jack, Queen, and King. Note that on this card—the Queen of Hearts—there is a small Q with a small heart underneath it. This is called the card index, and it signifies the card's value.

On the right is an example of a number card. The example shown is a Six of Spades. Once again, there is a card index in the upper left and the bottom right of the card. The six hearts in the middle of the card are called Pips. The number of card pips will match the value of the card.

Card Basics

Squaring the deck. Squaring the deck simply means making the deck even on both sides and even on the top and bottom. You can do this with one hand or two hands. To square the deck with one hand, place the deck in the palm of your left hand. Push on the sides of the deck, with your thumb on the left side and your fingers on the right side. Now take your index finger and hold the cards at the top of the deck, while pushing the cards with your little finger so they are even at the bottom of the deck.

To square the deck with two hands, hold the deck in the palm of your left hand and push the sides together, with your thumb on one side and your fingers on the other. Now, put your right hand over the cards. Place your right thumb at the bottom of the deck and your fingers at the top of the deck. Push the cards until they are even on the sides and on the top and bottom.

Spreading the cards. A deck of cards is often spread out to make it easy for a spectator to choose a card or to show that the cards have been shuffled. In certain card tricks, it may be necessary to spread the cards to show that certain cards are reversed or have changed color. To spread out the cards, begin with the deck in the palm of your left hand. Place the thumb of your right hand on top of the deck near the center. Place the other fingers of the right hand under the deck. Apply a little pressure with your right thumb on top and your right index finger on the bottom. Take your left thumb and push the upper part of the top card to the right. Keep using your left thumb to move the cards to the right—this will spread the cards out. This can be done with the faces down (with the backs showing) or the faces up.

Ribbon Spread. A Ribbon Spread is used to spread the entire deck out on a surface, such as a table. This is a good way to show all the card faces. Sometimes it is difficult to spread the cards evenly on a slick surface, such as a glass table. This is why many magicians use a close-up mat that makes it easier to spread out the cards. With practice, however, you can master the Ribbon Spread on any type of surface. To do the Ribbon Spread, take the deck from your left palm by placing your right hand on top of the deck. Do this with your right thumb at the back of the deck and your middle, ring, and little fingers holding the front of the deck. Place your right index finger on the left side of the deck. Place the cards down on the surface where you want to spread the cards. Now, as you move the deck of cards to the right, use your right index finger to space out the cards while you move them from left to right. Practice this very slowly at first. Soon, you will be able to impress your audience by spreading out the cards like a Las Vegas dealer!

Card Basics—The Ribbon Spread

To do the Ribbon Spread, set the deck on the table with your right hand. Put your right thumb on the back of the cards and your middle, ring, and little finger on the other side of the cards. Use your right index finger to slide the deck to the right. As you do this, gently raise your right finger, and the cards will stay in place. Practice this until you can do it smoothly.

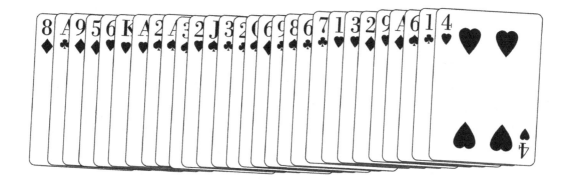

This illustration shows what a Ribbon Spread looks like when it is complete.

Card Basics—The Thumb Fan

The Thumb Fan. The Thumb Fan is another way to show all the cards in the deck. It is a card flourish (fancy card handling), and it will make your card routine look professional.

To do the Thumb Fan, hold the deck of cards, face up, in your left hand, as shown in the illustration on the left. Hold the cards with your fingers on the back of the deck and your thumb on the face of the deck. Put your left thumb near the bottom at about the center of the deck. Now, place your right thumb on the side of the cards at the left upper corner of the deck. Start pushing the cards over from left to right. Slowly but in one continuous motion, move the cards in a clockwise motion until the card index shows on all the cards. Practice this until you can do it smoothly. The card index corners should show evenly throughout the fan, as shown in the illustration on the right.

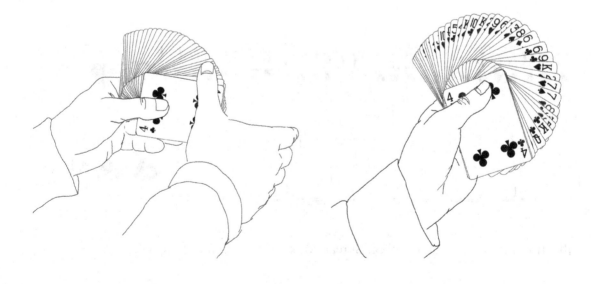

Cutting the cards. There are several ways to cut the cards. In the most basic method, a portion of the cards are taken off the top of the deck and then placed on the bottom. You can do this cut yourself, or you might want a spectator to do it. Most people know what to do when you ask, "Would you like to cut the cards?" Using some of the more advanced methods to cut the cards is a great way to begin a card routine. The One-Handed Cut is a good example of this.

False Cuts. A false cut is a technique that is used to make it appear as if the deck has been cut but actually, the cards are in the original order. As a blind magician, I often use a False Cut. The method I use is very simple. I have the spectator make three or four stacks of cards. I then pick up the cards in a manner that appears as if the cards have been cut and mixed up. However, I simply make sure that the card that I want to control stays on the top or bottom as I place the packets on top of each other. There are many advanced techniques to make a False Cut. After you master basic card moves, you might want to learn more advanced sleight of hand techniques.

Overhand Shuffle. The Overhand Shuffle is probably the most widely used method to shuffle the cards. A shuffle is used to mix up the order of the cards. To do the overhand shuffle, hold the deck of cards in your right hand between your thumb and fingers. Use your left hand, palm up, to hold the bottom of the cards as you begin to shuffle. Lift about half the cards up with your right hand by placing pressure on them with your thumb and fingers. Your left hand will support the remaining cards. Now, let about half of the cards in your right hand fall in front of the cards in your left hand. Lift up the remaining cards in your right hand and place them in front of the cards that are now in your left hand. Repeat this movement several times. Practice this movement slowly at first, until you are comfortable with the technique.

The Riffle Shuffle. Another popular way to shuffle the cards is the Riffle Shuffle. To do a Riffle Shuffle, place the cards on a flat surface. Take about half of the deck, and place the top half in your right hand between your thumb and your middle and ring fingers. Now, do the same with the cards in your left hand. With the thumbs facing each other, raise up the ends of the cards by "springing" them—that is, hold the ends of the cards with your index fingers, and let the cards mix together by letting the cards alternate as you release the pressure with your thumbs. It may take a little practice to do this shuffle correctly, but it is well worth the practice time when you master it.

False Shuffle. The False Shuffle makes it appear as though the cards are being thoroughly shuffled when, in fact, the magician is controlling the cards to achieve a certain order. Usually, I do a simple False Shuffle to keep my key card on the top or bottom of the deck. This can be performed like the Overhand Shuffle, except instead of lifting up the entire back portion of the deck, you let the bottom card stay on the bottom, while lifting the other cards. Repeat this over and over, and the bottom card will remain on the bottom. When performed correctly, it is almost impossible to detect when the False Shuffle has been done.

The Key Card Principle. The Key Card Principle is used in a wide variety of card tricks. Using a key card simply means that you know what the card is and where it is located. The most basic way of learning a key card is to simply glimpse at the card on the top or bottom of the deck. To glimpse the bottom card on the deck, just slightly tilt the deck forward as you square up the cards. Do this casually and without calling attention to it. You can also use the top card on the deck as a key card. This can be done while spreading out the deck to show the spectator that the cards are shuffled. As you spread the face up cards in your hands, simply note the card that is all the way to the left. This will, of course, be the top card when you turn the deck face down. Once you know the top or bottom card, you are ready to perform a variety of card tricks.

Card Basics—The Key Card Principle

The Key Card Principle is used in many card tricks. An easy way to glimpse at the Key Card is to look at the bottom card as you pull the deck out of the box. Do this naturally and without calling attention to what you are doing.

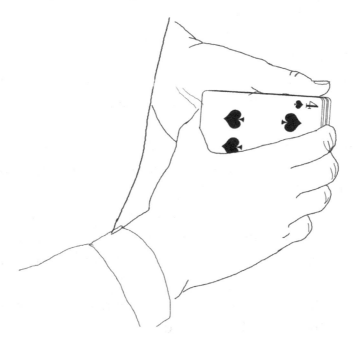

As shown above, you can glimpse at the Key Card after the deck has been shuffled. When the deck is handed back to you, simply tilt the cards away from you and look at the bottom card. Do this quickly and naturally.

To Perform a Trick Using the Key Card Principle

BOTTOM KEY CARD
1) Have a spectator shuffle the cards. When he hands you the cards, casually tilt them out so you can glimpse at the bottom card.
2) Have the spectator select a card. Tell him to remember the card and to replace it on top of the deck.
3) Have the spectator cut the cards and put the bottom half on top of the other portion of cards. This puts the Key Card directly on top of the spectator's chosen card. If you were to turn the cards face up and spread the deck, the chosen card would be directly to the right of the Key Card.

TOP KEY CARD
1) Have a spectator shuffle the cards. When he hands you the cards, spread them out, face up, between your hands and casually glimpse the card that is farthest to the left. (This will be the top card when you turn the deck face down.)
2) Have the spectator make four (or any number) piles of cards. Keep track of which pile has the Key Card on top.
3) Tell the spectator to choose one of the piles of cards and to look at and remember the bottom card.
4) Pick up the pile of cards that has the chosen card in it and put it on top of the pile that has the Key Card on top. This places the chosen card directly on top of the Key Card.
5) Place the remaining piles of cards on top of the two piles of cards from Step 4.
6) If you turn the cards face up and spread them between your hands, the chosen card will be directly to the left of the Key Card.
Note: If the spectator selects the pile of cards that has the Key Card on top, then simply cut the packet and complete the cut. This will put the chosen card directly on top of the Key Card. Place all the other piles of cards on top, as before.

Because I cannot see the cards, I usually cut the cards so that my Key Card is on the top or bottom of the deck. However, you will be able to just look at the card to know where it is.

You Do It!

This is an easy to do, self-working card trick. As a blind magician, this is one of my favorite tricks. I am often asked, *"How can you do a card trick if you can't see the cards?"* In this trick, you don't have to see the cards. Even more amazing, you don't even touch the cards.

Effect: A spectator's chosen card is revealed magically by the spectator himself.

Setup: There is no setup required for this trick.

Performance: You say, *"I would like to perform a card trick in which I never touch the cards."*

Say to a spectator, *"Please shuffle the deck of cards until you are satisfied that they are thoroughly mixed up."* Let the spectator take as much time as he wants to shuffle the cards.

Then you say, *"Good. Now I would like you to cut the cards approximately in half. Please look at the bottom card from the top half, and remember it. Now replace the top half back on the bottom half."*

"I would now like you to make four piles of cards. Deal out one card to each pile and alternate from pile to pile. Do this until you have dealt out all the cards." (When he has finished, the spectator will have four piles of cards on the table.)

"I would now like you to go through each pile until you find your card. Do not disturb the order of the cards. When you see your card, set that pile of cards in front of you."

"I now want you to slowly turn over the cards, face up, as you spell a magical word. In fact, the word is 'MAGICAL.' Spell it as you turn over a card for each letter." (The spectator spells out the word.) *"Believe it or not, you really have done something magical. Turn over the next card."*

When the spectator turns over the card, it will be his chosen card!

Remember that the magician (that's you) has never touched the cards, and the spectator has shuffled the cards before the start of the trick.

Note: Any seven-letter word will work for this trick. You might want to use the person's name if it has seven letters in it, or use a company name if you are doing this for a company party.

No-Problem Card Location

This is a great trick, and it is very easy to learn. It makes use of the Key Card Principle explained in Card Basics. I use a "pegged card" to do this trick, but you will be able to do it without prepared cards. I am sure this easy to learn trick will become one of your favorites!

Effect: A spectator freely selects a card from the deck. After memorizing the card and showing it to the audience, he places the card on top of the deck. The magician asks the spectator to cut the cards anywhere he chooses. The magician explains about the term "poker face"—that some people are very good at hiding their facial expressions as to what their cards are. Some people do not have a very good poker face and react in a unique way when they see certain cards. He says that he will use this to determine the spectator's card. He tells the spectator to say the name of each card as it is shown but not to make any expression or sound that will give away the identity of his chosen card or that will let the magician know when the spectator sees his card. The magician takes the deck and begins to slowly deal the cards, face up, on the table. The spectator says the name of each card. When the spectator's card appears, the magician immediately exclaims, *"That's your card!"*

Setup: There is no setup required for this trick. It uses the Key Card Principle (see Key Card Principle in Card Basics). All you need to do is to catch a glimpse of the bottom card before you start the trick. This is done naturally by slightly tilting the cards toward you. Remember the card. (As a blind magician, I make sure I know what the bottom card is before I take the deck of cards out of the card case.)

Performance: As you take the cards out of the case, take a look at the bottom card. Do this naturally and without bringing any attention to it. Hold the cards face down in your left hand. Use the thumb of your right hand to hold down the cards. Use your left thumb to spread out the cards. Do this by pushing the tops of the cards, left to right. Tell the spectator, *"Please select a card."* At this point, I turn my head to the side to make a point that I am not looking at the cards—this makes the audience feel that the spectator is not being influenced to select any particular card.

Now say, *"Please remember your card, and show it to the audience. Now place it on top of the deck. Good! Now cut the cards anywhere you want."* The spectator will cut the cards by lifting off a portion of the cards. The cut is completed by placing the bottom portion of the cards on top of the portion of cards the spectator lifted off. This will place the Key Card directly on top of the spectator's chosen card.

After the spectator cuts the cards, say, *"Have you ever heard about someone who did not have a very good poker face? It is used to describe the look a person gets when he sees a certain card. For example, a person might get a certain expression on his face if he sees a card that is needed for a good poker hand."* At this point, I explain that because I am blind, I listen for rapid breathing or unusual changes in the voice instead of looking for facial expressions. You might even use the story of knowing a blind magician whose hearing was so good that he could hear when a person was rapidly breathing.

Now say, *"I am now going to turn over the cards, face up, one by one, and I want you to name that card. If the card is a Four of Hearts, I want you to say, 'Four of Hearts.' Say it clearly and loud enough for the audience to hear. Do not change your tone of voice when you see your card or do anything that will alert me to what your card is."* Slowly start to deal out the cards, face up, one at a time, on the table.

The spectator will name the cards. When he names the Key Card (the card you originally glimpsed on the bottom of the deck), you will automatically know that the next card will be the spectator's chosen card.

When the spectator's card is shown, immediately say *"That's your card!"*

No-Problem Card Location

This illustration shows you how to glimpse the bottom card when you are taking the cards out of the box. The bottom card will be your Key Card.

Five Times Five Equals Magic!

This is a self-working card trick that requires no sleight of hand or complicated techniques. Remember, the key to magic is in the presentation. Practice your routine until you are confident and feel relaxed when you perform it.

Effect: A spectator shuffles the deck of cards and freely cuts the deck into five separate piles. The spectator is asked to select any pile and look at the bottom card. The spectator looks at the bottom card and sets the pile back down on the table. The magician then takes two piles of cards and puts them on the top of the spectator's pile and then puts two piles of cards on the bottom of the spectator's pile. The magician asks the spectator to freely cut the deck anywhere he chooses. The magician then spreads the cards to help him get a "mental image" of the card. The magician squares up the deck of cards and taps the cards five times with his fingers. He then dramatically announces the spectator's card!

Setup: No setup is required for this trick. This trick uses the Key Card Principle (Top Key Card) that I explained in Card Basics. This trick can be done with a borrowed deck, and it can be shuffled before you start the trick. As a blind magician, I do this trick by knowing what the Key Card is before I perform the trick. You will be able to glimpse the Key Card after it has been shuffled.

Performance: Have a spectator shuffle the deck. When the deck is handed back to you, spread out the cards (face up) between your hands. Tell the spectator you want to make sure the deck is shuffled thoroughly. While doing this look at the card that is farthest to the left. This will be the top card when you turn the cards face down (see illustration). This is the Key Card. Glimpse the card naturally, and do not call any attention to it. Make a mental note of the Key Card.

Say, *"Please make five piles of cards. The number of cards you use in each pile is a completely free choice, but use all the cards in the deck."*

Remember which pile has the Key Card on top. As the Key Card was on the top of the deck, this will be the first pile of cards the spectator sets down on the table.

Say, *"Good. Now select any one of the piles, and look at the bottom card and remember it. Do not tell me what it is, but you may show it to the audience. You may not know it, but by selecting this particular pile of cards, you have given it magical powers. How did it feel?"* (The spectator and the audience will find this amusing.) *"I will now place a pile of cards on top of your pile."*

Pick up one of the piles of cards—but not the pile with the Key Card on top—and place it on the spectator's chosen pile. Say, *"I will put these two piles on this pile."* Put the two piles of cards on top of the pile that has the Key Card on top. This action puts the spectator's chosen card directly on top of the Key Card.

"And I will put the two remaining piles of cards on the bottom of these cards." Do just that. Take the two remaining piles, and put them on the bottom of the cards you are holding

Note: If the spectator selects the pile of cards that has the Key Card on top, have him cut the cards in that pile. This will put the Key Card on the bottom of the spectator's chosen card. You can then pick up the remaining cards the same way as above.

Square up the deck of cards and say, *"Please cut the cards anywhere you like."* Take the deck of cards, and spread them in your hands. Thumb through the cards until you see your Key Card. (If you thumb the cards from left to right, the spectator's chosen card will be immediately to the left of the Key Card) Make a mental note of the spectator's card but do not call attention to it. Keep thumbing through the cards naturally.

Say, *"Hm-m-m ... I will need your help. Please tap the deck of cards five times with your finger. Good—that helps."* This has nothing to do with the trick but helps to build up the presentation. Slowly say, *"You chose the ___ (say the name of the chosen card).* Act as surprised as the audience!

Five Times Five Equals Magic!

When the spectator hands you the cards, spread them out, face up, between your hands. Look at the card that is farthest to the left. This will be your Key Card. In this illustration, the Key Card would be the Ace of Diamonds.

Reverse Reveal-ation

This is a fun trick to do, and it is easy to learn. It requires no complicated moves, but your audience will find it very entertaining.

Effect: A spectator selects a card and puts it back anywhere in the deck. Magically, the card reverses itself in the deck!

Setup: There is no setup required.

Performance: Have a spectator thoroughly shuffle the cards. Then, without calling attention to it, reverse the bottom card (see illustration). I do this by simply bringing the cards down below the table and reversing the card. I do this naturally and immediately spread out the cards (face down) in my hands, being careful not to expose the reversed card on the bottom, to show the spectator that the cards are all face down. (Only I know that the bottom card is face up.)

Say, *"I would like you now to freely select any card in the deck. Remember this is a free choice. I will even give you an opportunity to change your mind if you are not satisfied with the card."* Have the spectator select a card, and if he wants, he can change it for another card. *"Please remember the card. Show it to the audience, but don't tell me what it is."*

When the spectator shows the audience the card, turn the deck over. Do this naturally and without calling any attention to it. Make sure you keep the deck squared up so you don't expose any of the face up cards that are under the only face down card, which is on the top.

Now say, *"Good. Place it back in the deck. Remember, you have a free choice of where you put it. I do not want to influence you in any way."* Keep the deck squared up, and let the spectator slip his face down card into the deck. I hold the deck slightly down and keep it squared up by using both hands.

At this point, tilt the cards to the side and *"accidentally"* let the top card (which is the reversed card) fall. Do this very naturally. You really don't have to say anything, but if you want, you can say, *"Oops! Sorry about that."* Then just naturally pick up the card and replace it on top of the deck. While dropping the card, turn the deck back over so that it is face down. (When you do this, the only card in the deck that is face up will be the spectator's chosen card.)

Say, *"Now please watch very closely."* Snap your fingers and spread the cards out on the table. (Use the Ribbon Spread, as described in Card Basics.) The spectator's chosen card will be the only face up card in the deck!

Reverse Reveal-ation

The illustration below (left side) shows how to turn over the bottom card on the deck. Do this out of sight of the audience. I just naturally drop the deck down below the table and turn the bottom card face up.

The illustration on the right shows how to "accidentally" drop the reversed card.

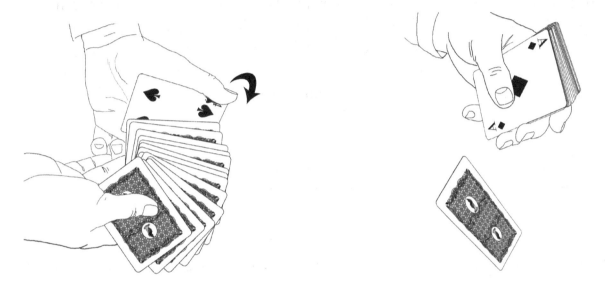

The illustration below shows how the spectator's chosen card will look, as it is the only face up card in the deck. The cards are in a Ribbon Spread on the table.

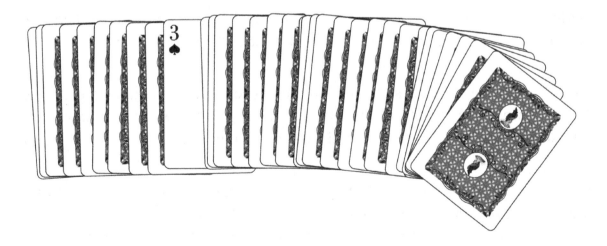

Four Sisters Reunion

This is a quick and easy trick. You will be able to do it in a matter of a few minutes. It is self-working, and there are no difficult moves to learn.

Effect: The magician takes the two red Queens out of the deck. He then deals out some cards until a spectator tells him to stop. He marks this location with one of the face up Queens. He then repeats the dealing process. Once again, the spectator says to stop. The magician marks this location with the other face up Queen. The magician spreads out the deck and takes out the two face up Queens, and the cards that are above the Queens. Amazingly, even though the spectator told the magician to stop in two random places, the face down cards are now turned over to reveal the two black Queens!

Setup: Put the Queen of Spades on top of the deck and the Queen of Clubs on the bottom. Do this before you perform the trick.

Performance: Go through the deck and find the two red Queens—Queen of Hearts and the Queen of Diamonds. Place them face up on the table. Tell the spectator, *"These two ladies have special powers. I am going to use them as marker cards. I am going to deal out the cards, and I want you to stop me when you feel like it. I will not influence you in any way."*

Begin dealing out the cards, one at a time, face down into a pile. When the spectator says to stop, say, *"Good. We'll mark it with one of our ladies."*

Place one of the red Queens face up, on the portion of cards you just dealt. Put the remaining cards on top of this portion. (Only you know that you have just put one of the black Queens on top of the face up Queen.)

Say, *"Let's do it one more time. Stop me at any point."* Do the same thing as above—deal out the cards until the spectator says to stop. *"Let's mark that spot with the other lady."* Put the other red Queen face up, on the pile of cards. Take the remainder of the cards and place them on top. (Only you know that you now have put the other black Queen on top of the face up Queen.)

Say, *"I told you that these ladies have special powers."* As you say this, fan out the deck until you see the first face up red Queen. Take it out, along with the card that is on top of it. Set the two cards down on the table. Now, continue fanning through the deck until you come to the other face up red Queen. Take it out, along with the card that is on top of it, and set them down on the table.

"The special power that the Queens have is that they always can find their sisters." Turn the face down cards over to reveal the other two Queens.

I Can Hear It Now!

This is one of the first tricks I learned. I like it because it is simple, and it can be used in any situation. It can be done with a borrowed, shuffled deck.

Effect: A spectator selects a card. The magician puts the deck of cards to his ear and listens to what the cards are "telling" him. Amazingly, the magician is able to reveal the spectator's chosen card.

Setup: No setup is required. As a blind magician, I have to know what the bottom card is before I perform the trick, or I must control a "known" card on the bottom. This, of course, will not be necessary for you.

Performance: Have a spectator shuffle the cards. Take the deck from the spectator. While showing that the cards are indeed shuffled, look at and remember the bottom card. For instructional purposes, let's say it is the Three of Diamonds. Hold your right thumb over the upper left portion of the bottom card. Your right hand will cover most of the bottom card, as shown in the illustration. (This action will hide the identity of the bottom card.) Do this naturally, and fan through the cards quickly.

Say, *"Good. The cards are shuffled. I will now pull back a few cards, and I would like you to stop me at any time."* The deck should be in the palm of your left hand. Place your right hand on top of the deck. Without calling attention to it, gently slide the bottom card toward you. Do this by sliding the deck forward with your right hand and keeping pressure on the bottom card with your left hand. (You don't need to jog it out too much—just enough so you can slide it back later).

With the middle finger of your right hand, pull back a few cards. Continue doing this as you slide back the cards from the top to the bottom. (Do this with the middle finger of your right hand.) Pull back a few cards at a time.

When the spectator says STOP, slide the upper portion back toward you. While doing this, slide the bottom card back, too. Use your right thumb to pull back the bottom card. ("Pinch" the top portion of cards and the bottom card together.)

Thus, when you separate the top portion from the bottom, the Three of Diamonds will still be on the bottom. Practice this move until you can do it smoothly.

Show the bottom card (only you know it is the Three of Diamonds) and say, *"Please remember your card."* Take the upper portion of the deck, and put it back on top of the bottom portion. At this point, you have *"forced"* a card on the spectator. (There are hundreds of ways to force a card, but this is one of the easiest.)

The rest of the trick is in how you build up the performance. Say, *"Over the many years of doing card magic, I have actually found a way to listen to what the cards are saying. It's something like a magician's Morse code. I know you think this is impossible, but please watch closely."* Hold the deck of cards up to your ear. Riffle the cards with your right thumb. Do this slowly by riffling just a few cards at a time. As you are still riffling the cards, say, *"Your card was ... the ...* (stop riffling the cards) *the ... Three of Diamonds. Is that correct?"* The spectator will agree in amazement, and your audience will be astonished at your ability to "listen to the cards."

I Can Hear It Now

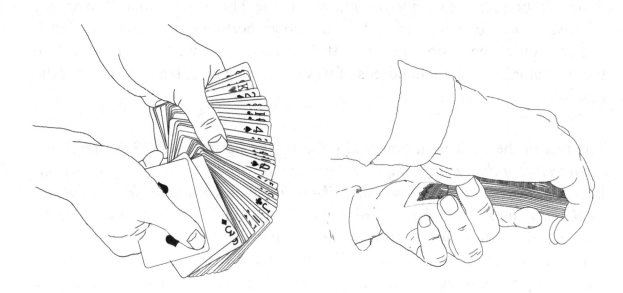

The illustration on the left shows you how to cover the value of the card using the thumb of your right hand. Casually look at the card before you spread out the cards. The bottom card will be your Key Card. The illustration on the right shows how to slide back the bottom card. Just slide it back about a half an inch.

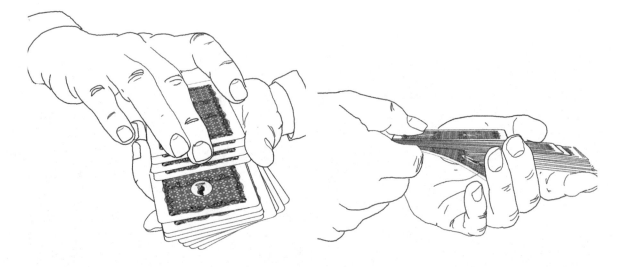

The illustration on the left shows you how to hold the cards in your left hand. Then use your right index finger to slide a few cards back. Keep sliding more cards back until the spectator says STOP.

The illustration on the right shows how to slide the bottom back as you are sliding the top portion of cards back. Pull off the top portion and bottom card in one smooth, continuous movement.

The Lie Detector Deck

This is a classic of card magic. It is listed in several different books and in courses on card magic. It is very easy to do and is an audience favorite.

Effect: A spectator freely selects a card and returns it to the deck. The magician then uses the deck of cards as a "lie detector" to reveal the spectator's chosen card.

Setup: There is no setup required for this trick. It uses the Key Card Principle (see Key Card Principle in the Card Basics section). As a blind magician, I make sure I know what the bottom card is before I perform the trick. You will not need to do this. You can perform the trick with a borrowed, shuffled deck.

Performance: Have a spectator thoroughly shuffle the cards. When the spectator hands you the cards, glimpse at the bottom card on the deck. This can be done by slightly tilting the cards away from you. Do not call attention to it, but just quickly look at the bottom card. This is the Key Card. Remember what it is.

Ribbon Spread the cards face down on the table. Say to the spectator, *"Please select any card you want. Look at it and show it to the audience, but do not tell me what it is. Are you satisfied with that card? If not, you may select another."* (By saying this, you remove any suspicion that the cards are somehow stacked or set up.) *"Make sure you remember your card."*

Pick up the cards as the spectator shows his card to the audience. Square up the deck and have the spectator place his card on top of the deck. Ask the spectator to cut the deck. Complete the cut by putting the bottom portion on the top portion of cards. (By doing this, you have put the Key Card directly above the spectator's chosen card.) You are now all set. All you have to do is add some dramatics to your performance.

Say, *"I am sure most of you have heard of a polygraph. It is more commonly known as a lie detector. I would now like to demonstrate how I can use a deck of cards in the same way."* Turn to the spectator and say, *"I will try to determine when you are lying just by listening to the different sounds in your voice.*

I will now turn my back. I want you to slowly deal out the cards, one at a time. Deal the cards face up and say out loud what the card is. However, when you come to your chosen card, call that card by a different name. So, if your card was the Jack of Diamonds just name a different card, like the Two of Spades or any other card. Tell the truth on what all the cards are except when you come to your card."

The spectator will deal out the cards face up and announce each card. As soon as the spectator comes to the Key Card you will know that the next card is his chosen card. As soon as he announces the next card after the Key Card say, *"Stop! That's a lie!"* Then turn around and act as surprised as your spectator and audience!

Telepathy Times Two

You will enjoy performing this easy to learn card trick. It requires no sleight of hand or complicated technique.

Effect: A spectator is asked to shuffle a deck of cards until he is satisfied that the cards are thoroughly mixed up. He is then asked to think of any number between one and ten. The spectator uses that number to count down from the top of the deck to see which card is at that position. The magician takes the cards and puts them behind his back. He then asks another spectator to name any number higher than ten. The magician announces that he will place the first spectator's chosen card at the position of the second spectator's number. The first spectator is given the deck of cards and told to count down to the number that the second spectator gave. Amazingly, the chosen card is at that particular location!

Setup: No setup is required for this trick. It can be done with a borrowed, shuffled deck.

Performance: A spectator is asked to thoroughly shuffle the cards. It is sometimes a nice touch to let a second spectator also shuffle the cards. This will eliminate any doubt about a setup or stacked deck.

Say, *"I would now like you to think of a number between one and ten. Remember, this is completely a free choice, and I do not want to influence you in any way."* For instructional purposes, let's assume the spectator says seven. Say, *"Good. Are you sure you want that number? If not, you can change your mind."* If he changes his mind, it only adds to the performance. Say, *"What is the number you chose?"* We'll assume he decided on seven. Say, *"Then seven it is. Count down seven cards from the top, and then look at and remember the seventh card. Do not show it to anyone, and do not tell me what it is. Do not change the order of the cards. Put the cards back on top of the deck."*

You now take the cards from the spectator and put them behind your back. Ask another spectator, *"Would you please think of any number between ten and twenty? You are free to choose any number, and I will not influence you in any way. What is your number?"* Let's assume the second spectator says fifteen.

Here's where the magic takes place. While the cards are behind your back, count off the number that the second spectator has announced. In our example, it was fifteen.

Count the cards out so you are putting one card on top of the other. In other words, put the second card on top of the first, the third on top of the second, and so on. By doing this, you are reversing the order of the cards. Now, put the cards you counted back on top of the deck. While you are doing this, say, *"I would like to magically place the first spectator's card at the number that the second spectator gave. I know it sounds impossible because there is no way I could know what number either of the spectators would select ... or the identity of the chosen card."*

Bring the cards out from behind your back and give them to the first spectator. Say, *"I would now like you to count out the cards to the number that was mentioned by the second spectator. And I would like you to start counting from the number you originally thought of, which was seven. Start counting at seven."* The spectator will count out the cards out loud. *"Seven, eight, nine,"* and so on until he gets to the number that was mentioned by the second spectator (which in our example was fifteen).

Say to the spectator, *"What was your selected card? Good. Now turn over the last card you dealt out."* It will be the chosen card!

Side by Side

This trick is self-working and requires no sleight of hand. It is said that the great Ed Marlo created it.

Effect: Two spectators are each given half the deck of cards. Each spectator chooses a number between one and ten. The magician then turns his back and asks the spectators to count out the number of cards they have chosen. They hide the cards so that the magician has no idea of the number of cards they've chosen. The magician then takes one portion of the deck and counts out all the cards. The spectator remembers the card that corresponds to the number of cards he chose. This same procedure is done for the second spectator. The cards are set on a table side by side. The spectators are asked which card they each chose. The magician starts turning over the cards of each pile. The spectators' cards magically show up side by side.

Setup: No setup is required for this trick.

Performance: Ask two spectators from the audience to help you with this trick. Count (silently to yourself) twenty-six cards and hand them to the first spectator. Hand the rest of the deck to the second spectator. (I try to count out the cards in small groups of three and four cards, while still keeping track of counting to twenty-six. I think this is a good way to not call any attention to the fact you are counting to a certain number.)

Say, *"You both have about half the cards in the deck. I would now like you to both think of a number from one to ten. It is important that you each have a different number. It is also important that you don't let me know which number you choose. I'll turn away so that you can decide which numbers you want to choose. You can show each other with your fingers or write the numbers on a piece of paper. After you both have chosen a different number, I would like you to deal off that number of cards from those that you are holding. Do it quietly so there is no way I can know the number of cards you choose. Then I would like you to hide the cards you chose. You can hold them under the table or put them in your pocket. Let me know when you're done."*

After they have hidden their cards, turn back around. Take the cards from the first spectator. These are the cards that he didn't count out. Say to the first spectator, *"I am now going to turn these cards over, face up. I will count out the cards. I want you to remember the card that falls at the place of the number of cards you chose. Just remember the card, and don't say anything out loud that will call attention to the identity of that card."*

I usually go through the motions of what I am going to do to make sure the spectator knows what he needs to do. Slowly turn the cards over, face up, while counting, *"One, two, three ..."* Stop counting out loud when you get to ten, and silently count out three more cards. (You will have thirteen cards counted out in a face up pile when you are done. It is important to count out thirteen cards for the trick to work). Ask the first spectator, *"Did you remember the card that was at your number?"* If he says yes, proceed with the trick. If he says no, turn the pile of face up cards over, and count them out again in the same way as described. Turn the face up pile of cards face down, and then put the remaining cards on top of the pile. Set the cards down on the table.

Say to the second spectator, *"And now we will do the same thing for you."* Go through the same procedure as you did with the first spectator. Tell the second spectator to remember the card that falls at the number of cards he chose. As before, stop counting out loud at ten, but silently count out thirteen cards. You will now have two stacks with thirteen cards each. Turn the cards face down, and place the rest of the cards on top. Set this pile of cards next to the other pile of cards. The cards are now Side by Side.

Now for some dramatics: Snap your fingers over each pile of cards. Then tap the top of the cards with your finger. Hesitate after doing this, as if you are in deep thought and studying the cards. Say to the first spectator, *"What was the name of your card? Please say it loud enough so it can be heard by everyone in the audience."*

Repeat the name of the card that the first spectator says aloud. Then say to the second spectator, *"And now, what was your card? Please tell everyone."* Repeat the name of his card also.

Say, *"When we first started, you each chose a different number. Wouldn't it be a miracle if somehow, someway, the cards you chose turned up at the exact same place in these piles of cards?"*

Slowly turn over the top card of each pile, and then continue to turn over each card at the same time. While you are doing this, repeat the names of the cards that the spectators chose. When you get to the chosen cards, stop and act as amazed as the audience!

Jacks or Better

This is one of my favorite tricks. Your audience will be amazed by this great yet easy to learn trick.

Effect: This is a transposition trick in which four Jacks trade places with the four Aces.

Setup: No setup is required for this trick. As a blind magician, I ask someone to take out the four Jacks and four Aces for me. Of course, you will be able to take them out of the deck for yourself. If I use this trick as an opener, I simply have the four Jacks and four Aces on top of the deck.

Performance: Spread out the cards, face up on the table. Remove the four Jacks and set them aside. Now place the face up deck on top of the four face up Jacks. Spread out the deck again, and take out the four Aces. Set them down, and place the rest of the face up deck on top of the four Aces.

Pick up the deck, and turn it face down. You now have the four Aces on top of the deck, with the four Jacks underneath the Aces. Spread the cards, and take seven cards but make the audience think you are taking eight cards. If you do this rather quickly, the audience will never suspect that you actually take only seven cards. Say, *"We have four Aces and four Jacks."* Count out the four Jacks, but make it only look as if you are counting out the four Aces. You actually leave a Jack on top of the deck.

Take the packet of seven cards (remember that the audience assumes you have eight cards in the packet) with your right hand, and put the rest of the deck down on the table.

Put the packet of cards in your left hand. Take off the top card and place it on the bottom of the packet. Say, *"One, two, three, four Aces, and one, two, three, four Jacks."* As you say this, take the card from the top of the packet, and put it on the bottom. When you get to the fourth Jack it will actually be an Ace but the audience will assume it is a Jack. That's how the trick works. Select a spectator from the audience to help you. As you name the "fourth Jack" put it down on the table and say to the spectator, *"Hold your finger down on this Jack."* (You are actually giving him an Ace.)

Repeat this counting method. *"One, two, three, four Aces, and one, two, three Jacks. Hold this Jack down, too."* Place this *"Jack"* in the spectator's hand and have him hold down the cards with his finger.

Again count out the cards. *"One, two, three, four Aces and one, two Jacks. Please hold this Jack also."*

Now we have one, two, three, four Aces and one Jack." Have the spectator take the final *"Jack"* and place it on top of the rest of the *"Jacks"* (Actually, the spectator is now holding the four Aces). The spectator will assume that you are holding the four Aces, but you are actually holding only three Jacks.

Take the cards in the packet, and put them back on top of the deck. (You have now placed three Jacks on top of the Jack that was originally left on top of the deck.)

Now say, *"I'll give you a hundred dollars if you can tell me which of your cards is the Jack of Diamonds."* No matter what card the spectator turns over, it will be an Ace. Now, have him turn over the other cards to show that the four Jacks are now four Aces!

High Voltage

You will enjoy learning this fun and easy to do trick. It is self-working and is an audience favorite. It is another trick that uses the Key Card Principle.

Effect: The magician explains the principle of static electricity and offers to use a deck of cards to demonstrate it. A spectator is asked to shuffle a deck of cards. He is then asked to freely select a card. The magician asks the spectator to "charge" up the card by rubbing it vigorously. The card is then returned to the top of the deck, and the cards are cut. The magician spreads out the cards on the table and proceeds to touch the cards with his finger. He comes to one card, and it gives him an "electric shock." It is the spectator's chosen card.

Setup: No setup is required. The trick uses the Key Card Principle which I explained in Card Basics. As a blind magician I need to know what the Key Card is before the performance.

Performance: Explain the nature of static electricity. Say, *"Have you ever received a shock from touching a door knob after walking on a carpet? That is static electricity. Static electricity is the buildup of electricity on an object. Touching the object causes the electricity to be discharged, and we get a small shock. I would like to demonstrate this principle by using this deck of cards."* Any deck of cards can be used.

Have the spectator shuffle the deck. When he hands it back to you, glimpse (look at) the bottom card. Do this very naturally and without calling attention to it. You can glimpse the card by tilting it slightly away from you when the spectator hands you the cards. This bottom card is the Key Card. For instructional purposes, let's say the bottom card is the Two of Diamonds.

Spread the cards and say, *"Please select a card and remember it. You may show it to the audience, but do not tell me what it is."* Let's assume the spectator selects the Jack of Spades. *"Now I would like you to vigorously rub the card to charge it up with static electricity."* This has nothing at all to do with the trick but helps in building up the presentation. *"Place the card on top of the deck. Be careful, as it is now fully charged up with electricity.*

Good. Now I would like you to freely cut the cards anywhere you choose." In doing this the spectator will be putting his chosen card directly under the Key Card.

Take the cards and spread them out on the table, face up. When you come to the Two of Diamonds you will see that the spectator's chosen card is immediately to the right. (This is if the deck has been spread out left to right.) Don't call attention to the chosen card yet.

I use my finger to sort through the cards as though I am expecting to get "shocked" at any moment. I spread out the cards to make sure the audience can see the Jack of Spades but I don't call attention to it yet. I now act as if I am going back through the cards, and when I touch the Jack of Spades I act as if I have been shocked by electricity. I usually lift my hand up quickly and shake it vigorously. I then say, *"Wow! You really charged it up!"* I then push the spectator's chosen card forward on the table, but I do it in a way that shows I think I might be shocked again.

Note: At one time I would do this trick with an Atomic Light bulb. The Atomic Light is a magic prop that can be obtained from most magic dealers. It looks like a regular 60-watt light bulb, but it can be turned on and off at any time as you hold it in your hand. I would bring out the bulb at the end of the presentation and turn it on when I touched the spectator's chosen card. It was as if the "electricity" in the spectator's card had turned on the light bulb. This variation might be something you'll want to add to the presentation at some time in the future.

The Royal Treatment

Your audience will love this self-working card trick!

Effect: The magician talks about the big poker games that are on television. He explains that it would be nice to somehow influence the dealer so that he would be dealt a winning hand. He deals five poker hands to different spectators and comments that they probably wouldn't be too good in a high-stakes poker game. The magician gathers up the cards and hands them to one of the spectators. He then has the spectator deal out the hands of cards to the others and a hand to the magician. The spectators' cards are shown, but the real magic is in the magician's cards. He has a Royal Flush!

Setup: To set up this trick, put a Royal Flush (Ten, Jack, Queen, King and Ace of Spades) on top of the deck. Mix up the order of the flush. You don't want it to be obvious that the cards were stacked before the trick.

Performance: The magician (that's you) deals five poker hands of five cards each to five different spectators. Each hand will have one card of the Royal Flush in it. Say, *"I am sure some of you have seen the poker tournaments that are now very popular on TV. It is interesting that some players will try to bluff when they really don't have a good hand. I am sure they get excited when they get a good hand."* At this point you can comment on the cards that the spectators are holding. *"Some of you would probably fold immediately with the hand you have, while some of you might want to stay in the game."*

At this point, gather up the cards, making sure to pick them up in the following manner: Pick up each hand, making sure to put the card that is part of the Royal Flush at the bottom. Place this hand of cards on top of the deck. Do this same thing with each of the other poker hands.

Say, *"Maybe someone else can deal better hands than I have."* Give the deck to one of the spectators and say, *"I would like you to deal the cards, and I'll take the last hand."* The spectator will deal the five poker hands, and you will receive the fifth hand of cards. (Unknown to the spectator or the audience, you now have a Royal Flush).

Say, *"Turn your cards over, and see what kind of hand you have."* Point to each spectator, one by one, and have him turn his cards face up for everyone to see.

"Now let's see what you dealt me." Slowly and dramatically turn your cards face up. Arrange them in the 10-Jack-Queen-King-Ace order and say, *"It must be my lucky day. I have a Royal Flush!"*

Pushed-Out Prediction

This is a quick and easy way to find a spectator's chosen card and is a unique way to glimpse the Key Card. You will enjoy performing this trick!

Effect: A spectator shuffles a deck of cards. The magician pushes out a middle portion of cards from the deck. The spectator selects a card. The deck is then cut and magically, the magician reveals the spectator's chosen card in a very unusual way.

Setup: There is no setup required for this trick. It may be done with a borrowed deck that has been shuffled.

Performance: Have the spectator shuffle the cards. Take the deck in your left hand, and hold the cards tilted outward. Use a pen or pencil to push out a middle portion of cards. Without calling attention to it, glimpse the bottom card of the top portion. This is your Key Card.

Say to the spectator, *"Please pull out the top card of the middle portion, and look at it. Remember it, and slide it back on top of the middle portion."* Slide the middle portion back so that the deck is squared up. (Only you know that you have now put the Key Card directly above the spectator's card). For instructional purposes, let's say the spectator's card is the Ten of Diamonds.

Say, *"Would you please cut the cards. Would you like to cut them again?"* I feel that asking this question adds to the performance. With the deck of cards in your hand, say, *"I would now like to reveal what your card is in a very unique way."*

Fan through the cards and find your Key Card. If you fan the cards left to right, the spectator's card will be directly to the right of the Key Card. Do not stop fanning the cards. Go through the entire deck so as not to call attention to the fact that you already know the spectator's chosen card.

Say, *"I would like you to concentrate on just the color of your card. Just the color and nothing else."* Because you already know that the spectator chose the Ten of Diamonds go through the deck and pull out *ANY* red card. Do not show it to the spectator yet. Hold the card up to your forehead, as though you are concentrating very intensely. Say, *"I think your card was a red card. Is that correct?"* Of course the spectator will agree with you.

Say, *"I would now like you to just concentrate on whether your card was a number card or a face card."* Once again, go through the deck and select *ANY* number card. Just make sure it is a different number than the one the spectator chose. Hold it up to your head and say, *"Yes, I think your card was a number card. Is that correct?"*

Then say, *"And now for the hard part of this trick. I would like you to think of your card in its entirety."* Go through the deck. Do not immediately take out the spectator's card. Instead, fan through the deck to make it look as if it's difficult to make your selection. Finally, take out the spectator's card. Hold it to your head and ask, *"Was your card ... the Ten of Diamonds?"* When the spectator confirms his card, slowly turn the card face up to reveal the spectators chosen card.

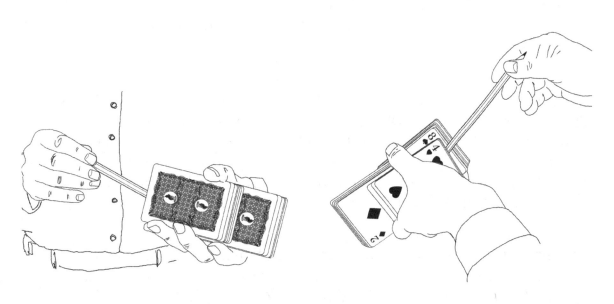

The illustration on the left shows you how to push out the middle portion of cards with the pencil.
The illustration on the right is the same as above but from the magician's view. This shows how to glimpse the card that is on the bottom of the top portion of cards. This will be your "prediction" card. In this illustration, the prediction card is the Eight of Spades.

Double-Decker Prediction

Although this particular trick uses two decks, it is very simple. It does not require complicated sleight of hand. As a blind magician, I like this trick because of its simplicity. Your audience will really enjoy it!

Effect: The magician asks a spectator to cut the deck of cards on the table. This is a completely free choice by the spectator. The magician then pulls another deck out of his pocket. He spreads the cards and shows that one card is reversed. Amazingly, it matches the card in the first deck where the spectator made the cut.

Setup: Two decks of cards are required for this trick. Before performing the trick, take the first deck and reverse any card in the middle of the deck. Put this deck of cards in your pocket. Now, take the second deck of cards and find the same card you reversed in the first deck. Put this card on top of the deck.

Performance: Select a spectator from the audience. Show the spectator the second deck of cards. (Only you will know what the top card is). Say, *"I would like you to cut the cards somewhere near the middle of the deck. This is a completely free choice, and I will not influence you in any way. Set the top portion that you cut off next to the rest of the deck."*

Take the bottom portion of cards and place it on top of the top portion that the spectator cut off. Set the lower portion at a 45-degree angle on top of the top portion. This will make it appear as though you are marking the place that the spectator cut. Actually, you are doing this to "force" a card. You will later lift up the angled portion of cards and show the top card of the bottom portion. This is the card you selected earlier, before the performance.

Take the first deck of cards out of your pocket. Spread the cards out on the table. Act surprised when you show that one card is reversed. Say, *"Wow! One card is face up. This has to be a special prediction of some kind."*

Point to the deck of cards that the spectator cut. Say to the spectator, *"Please turn over the top card on the bottom stack of cards."* It will match the reversed card in the second deck!

Double-Decker Prediction

The illustration on the left shows how to reverse a card and put it in the middle of the deck. In this illustration, the reversed card is the Four of Clubs, but you can make the prediction card any card you desire. This deck of cards will be your "prediction" and is placed in your pocket.

Now go through another deck of cards and find the same card as your prediction card. Put this card on the bottom of the deck. After the spectator cuts the cards from his deck of cards, set the bottom portion of cards on top of the other portion of cards, as shown in the lower corner of the illustration. Set the cards on top at an angle so they will be easy to pick up when you need to show the spectator where he cut the cards. (Only you know that the matching card is now on the bottom of the top portion of cards.)

The illustration on the right shows how to pick up the top portion of cards to show the spectator his chosen card.

X Marks the Spot

Although this trick is easy to do, it plays big to an audience. This trick requires no sleight of hand and no complicated moves.

Effect: The magician selects two spectators from the audience. He hands the deck of cards to the first spectator and also hands him a felt-tip marker. The magician tells the spectator to put the face up cards behind his back, select a card, and write an X across the face with the marker. The spectator then mixes his marked card back into the deck. The second spectator is handed the cards, which are now face down. The second spectator is asked to put the cards behind his back, select a card, and mark an X on the back of it. The magician then hands the deck back to the first spectator and asks him to find his face up card. It is easy to find, as it has an X across the face. The first spectator takes the card and places it on the table. The second spectator is asked to go through the deck and take out the card he marked. When he goes through the deck, he will find that his card is missing. The only card missing from the deck is on the table. The magician has the first spectator turn over the card. It has an X on the back! Amazingly, it seems both spectators selected and marked the same card!

Setup: For this particular trick, you will need to use a felt-tip marker that has been dried out and does not work. To do this, let the marker sit uncapped for a few days. Make sure it will not leave an ink mark. I leave the marker outside for a week and have always found it to be dried out sufficiently. You also might put clear fingernail polish on the dried-out marker. This will ensure that no ink will be put on the cards.

Before you begin the trick, remove any card from the deck. Use a marker (the same brand of marker as the marker you dried out) and put an X on both sides. Do not make the X too neat or too perfect. The trick calls for the spectator to make an X on the card while the cards are behind his back, so make the X as if it were made behind the back. Now place the card three cards down from the top of the deck. (This is done so you can spread out the cards without showing the marked card.)

Performance: Select two spectators from the audience. Hold the cards face up and spread them in your hands. (Do not spread them too far, as you do not want to reveal the marked card.) Say, *"I would like to show you that the cards are thoroughly mixed up."*

Say to the first spectator, *"I would like you to hold the cards face up behind your back and select a card. Put the card on top of the deck and mark an X across the face of the card."* (Use your finger to show the spectator how to make an X on the card. This will help him to know that you want the X big enough to go from one corner of the card to the other.) Give him the deck of face up cards and the marker. *"Once you have marked the X across the face of the card, place it somewhere back in the deck."*

Take back the deck and turn it face down. Say to the second spectator, *"I would like you to do the same thing, only I would like you to mark an X on the back of one card. Hold the cards behind your back, select a card, and put it on top. Mark the card with an X across the back of the card. Then put the card back somewhere in the deck."*

Take the cards and the marker from the second spectator. Put the marker away. Hold the cards face up. Say to the first spectator, *"I would like you to go through the deck and find your card. It will be easy to find because it will have your X on it. When you find the card, keep it face up and place it down on the table. Then put your hand over the card to cover it."* (This will keep the spectator from prematurely showing the back of the card.)

Say to the second spectator, *"I would now like you to go through the cards and find your card. It will be easy to find because it has your X on the back."*

The spectator will go through the deck a couple of times and then say that he can't find his card.

Say, *"Well, there is only one card that is missing from the deck, and that is the card under* (point to the first spectator) *your hand. Could you lift up your hand and turn over the card?"*

When the first spectator turns over the card, both spectators and the audience will be shocked to see that the back of the card has an X on it!

Say, *"Amazing! You both picked the same card!"*

X Marks the Spot

The illustration on the left shows how NOT to make the X on the card. It is too perfect, because if someone was writing an X on a card behind his back, it would not look like this.

The illustration on the right shows how an X would look on a card if someone were writing it behind his back. Practice writing an X on a card behind your back, and it will give you a good idea of how the X should look.

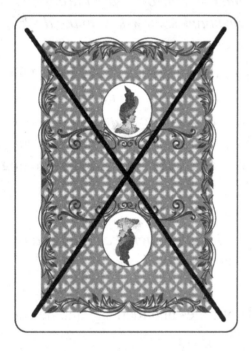 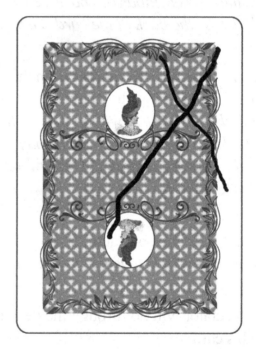

Yours and Mine

This is an audience favorite. It is easy to do, and you will enjoy learning it and performing it.

Effect: The magician (that's you) asks a spectator to cut the cards. The spectator takes half the deck and the magician keeps the other half. The magician and the spectator select a card from the cards they are holding and memorize the card. The magician inserts his card in the spectator's cards, and the spectator inserts his card in the magician's cards. The two halves of the deck are now put back together. The cards are then spread on the table to show that two cards are now face up. One is the spectator's card, and the other is the magician's card!

Setup: Before the performance, reverse the bottom card on the deck. Make sure to memorize it.

Performance: With the deck of cards in your left hand, say to the spectator, *"Please cut the cards so that you have about half, and leave me about half."*

Now say, *"Go through your cards and pick one out. Don't tell me what it is. I'll do the same thing."* Select a random card. It does not matter what it is, and you do not need to memorize it.

Say, *"Now put the cards in the palm of your left hand, and I will do the same. I will now put my chosen card face down in your packet of cards."* As you put your card into the spectator's packet, drop your left hand and turn over the packet, saying, *"I will ask you to put your card face down in my packet of cards."*

Be careful not to let the cards spread out to expose the now face up cards in your packet. The cards in your left hand will have the magician's reversed card, face down. The spectator's card, face down. And the rest of the packet, which will be face up. The audience, however, will assume the cards are all face down.

Say, *"Please cut your cards."* As the spectator cuts his packet of cards, drop your left hand and reverse your packet of cards. Say, *"Good. Now I'll cut my cards."* Do just that—cut your packet of cards.

"Now, put your packet of cards on top of mine. And just to really mix up the cards, why don't you cut them one more time?"

Here's the big finish. Say, *"I chose the _____* (name the card you originally reversed and put on the bottom of the deck)." And then ask the spectator, *"And what was your card?"*

After the spectator names his card, slowly spread out the cards on the table. Amazingly, there will be only two cards that are face up in the deck—one will be the card you selected, and the other will be the spectator's card.

Practice this trick until you can do it smoothly and in a relaxed manner. I think you will enjoy doing this trick as much as your audience will enjoy watching it!

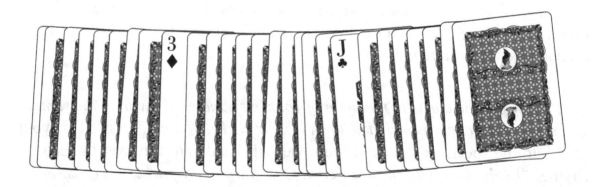

This illustration shows how the magician's selected card and the spectator's selected card look when the cards are in a Ribbon Spread at the finish.

Red-Black Revelation

This is a self-working prediction trick that you will enjoy performing. Practice it many times before you perform it—it will be a real audience pleaser.

Effect: The magician writes a prediction on a piece of paper. He folds it up and lays it on the table. He asks a spectator to thoroughly shuffle the cards and then to divide the deck approximately in half. The spectator keeps one half and gives the other half to the magician. After the spectator shuffles his half, he counts all the red cards in his half of the deck. Let's assume he counts eleven red cards. The magician then counts to the eleventh black card in his half of the cards—let's assume this is the Ace of Spades. The magician then tells the spectator to open the piece of paper on which he's written the prediction. It reads: You will select the Ace of Spades.

Setup: There is no setup required for this trick. It is important, however, that all fifty-two cards are in the deck.

Performance: Ask a spectator to thoroughly shuffle a deck of cards. Spread the cards out between your hands, as though you are studying the cards. Take this opportunity to remember the black card that is nearest to the top of the deck as you are looking at it. For instructional purposes, let's say this card is the Ace of Spades. Act as though you are in deep thought. Square up the deck and set it on the table. Then, on a piece of paper, write: *"You will select the Ace of Spades."* Fold the paper and put it on the table.

Pick up the deck of cards and count off the top twenty-six cards. This is half the deck. Give these cards to the spectator, saying, *"These are yours. Please shuffle them until you are completely satisfied they are thoroughly mixed up."*

"Good. Now please count the number of red cards you have." For instructional purposes, let's assume he says that he has eleven red cards. Say, *"Wow! Believe it or not, that number has a special magical quality to it. I will use it to count the black cards in my half of the deck."* Pick up the other half of the deck and count. Take the top card off of the face down deck and turn it face up. If this card is black say, *"One."* If the card is red, do not say anything. No matter what

color the card is, put it on the bottom of your half of the deck. Keep counting the black cards until you get to the eleventh black card. It will be the Ace of Spades. Say, *"Please open up and read the piece of paper on the table."* The spectator will read: *"You will choose the Ace of Spades."*

Cards of a Feather

This is a quick and easy to do trick. It requires no complicated moves. The real magic is in the presentation. Remember to practice repeatedly until you are confident with the handling and presentation.

Effect: A spectator shuffles the cards. He is then asked to cut the deck in half. The spectator takes half the deck, and the magician takes the other half. Each selects a card from his half and says what the card is. Magically, the magician causes his card to disappear from his half and to reappear next to the spectator's chosen card!

Setup: No setup is required. A deck may be borrowed, but it should be thoroughly shuffled. As a blind magician, I need to know what the Key Card is before I perform the trick. You, however, will not need to do this.

Presentation: Say to your audience, *"I'm sure you have heard the expression, 'Birds of a feather flock together.' It means that birds like to be with birds of the same species. I think cards like to do that too. Let me demonstrate."*

You may ask the spectator to shuffle the cards. When he hands you the deck, glimpse the bottom card. Do this naturally and without calling attention to the fact you are doing it. For instructional purposes, let's say the bottom card was the Two of Hearts. Remember the card. Set the cards on the table.

Say to the spectator, *"Please cut the cards in about half."* Once the spectator has done so, say, *"Good. Now you take half, and I'll take half."* The spectator takes the bottom half (the half with the Key Card on the bottom), and you take the top half.

Say, *"I would like you to go through the deck and freely select a card. Remember what it is, but don't tell me what it is. Then place your card on top of your half of the cards, and cut them one time."* Let's assume the spectator chose the King of Spades. Say, *"I'll do the same thing to my half of the cards."* Go through the cards and select any random card. It does not matter which card you select. Look at it, but you don't need to remember it. Place the card on top of your half of the cards, and cut them one time, just as the spectator did.

Now say, *"My card was the Two of Hearts. What was yours?"* After the spectator responds, then say, *"Please watch closely. I will now cause my card to disappear from my half of the cards."* As you say this, snap your fingers over the cards. Then spread out your cards to show the cards. If closely inspected, the Two of Hearts will not be there—it's as if it really disappeared. (Remember, this is the original Key Card).

"As I told you before, just as birds of a feather flock together, cards of a feather stick together." Snap your fingers over the spectator's cards and spread them out. The spectator and the audience will be amazed to see that the Two of Hearts is right beside the King of Spades which is the spectator's chosen card!

Six in the Mix

As a blind magician, this trick works well in my routine. You can perform it blindfolded! It is simple to do, and I am sure you will amaze and mystify your audience when you perform it.

Effect: The magician turns his back to the audience. For an even better effect, he is blindfolded. The magician shuffles the deck and while his back is turned, he asks a spectator to select a card and return it to the top of the deck. The spectator cuts the cards, and the magician shuffles the deck. The magician "feels" for a special energy coming from the deck. He selects a card and places it face down on the table. He then hands the deck of cards to the spectator. Then and only then does the magician turn around. If he is blindfolded, the blindfold is removed at this time. He asks the spectator to turn the card on the table face up. Let's say it is the Six of Spades. The magician explains that this was the "special energy" card. He tells the spectator to turn over six cards on top of the deck. When the spectator gets to the sixth card, it is his chosen card!

Setup: This is a trick that uses a pegged card. Use a safety pin or a paper clip to make a small indentation in the index of the Six of Spades as shown in the illustration. Hold the card facing you and slightly push the pin in the center of the card pip that is underneath the number six. This will create a small bump on the other side. I like to think of it as a Braille dot. Make it small enough so that it won't be easily noticed, but make sure you can feel it when you run your finger over it. Place the bump on both index corners of the card. Then, before you perform the trick, place this card so it is seven cards up from the bottom of the deck.

Presentation: Say to the audience, *"For this particular trick I will face away from you. You may even blindfold me if you wish."* Because I am blind, the audience thinks it's funny that I ask to be blindfolded, but this makes for a more dramatic performance. You can carry a bandana with you for a blindfold, and let the audience examine it. With your back to the audience and blindfolded, you now shuffle the cards. Use the False Shuffle (as explained in Card Basics). Let the audience see you "shuffle" the cards.

Say, *"I would now like you to freely select any card from the deck. Look at it and remember it, but don't tell me what it is. If you are not satisfied with the card, you may select another one."* Doing this removes any doubt that the spectator's chosen card was somehow "forced" on him. Say, *"Place your card back on top, and then please cut the cards."*

Take the cards back in your left hand. Run your right index finger over the cards near the upper right corner. Tell the audience, *"I will select a card that has a special energy."* Actually, you are feeling for the bump on the pegged card. This should be easy, as you know just about where the card was placed after the deck was cut. Feel the cards as though you are trying to feel the special energy. This will make this process look very natural. When you come to the pegged card, place it on the table. Say, *"Okay, I will use this card."* Take the cards that were above the pegged card and set them to one side. Give the remaining cards (the cards that were below the pegged card) to the spectator.

Now turn around to face the audience and if you have been blindfolded, take it off at this time. Say to the spectator, *"This card was trying to give me a message. It is telling me to use my sixth sense to find your card. The message was to have you turn the cards over, one by one, and stop on the sixth card."*

The spectator does exactly that and when he turns over the sixth card, it will be the card he selected!

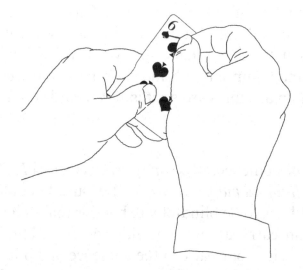

The illustration above shows how to use a pin or paper clip to punch a small hole in the corner index of the card. This will make a small bump on the back of the card, making it easy to feel with your finger or thumb. I like to think of it as a Braille dot, and it makes it easy for me to identify the card. I like using the Six of Spades, but you can use any card you like.

Six in the Mix

The illustration below shows where to place the pegged card (the Six of Spades). It should be placed seven cards up from the bottom of the deck. This is how it would look if the deck was face up and spread out.

The illustrations below and on the left show how the spectator cuts the cards. Remember that the spectator has selected a card from the deck and has placed it on top. Once he makes the cut, it will automatically place the pegged card (the Six of Spades) where it is seven cards above the selected card.

The illustration on the right shows how to use your finger to feel for the bump on the pegged card. As a blind magician, I have found that the pegged card can be very useful in card magic.

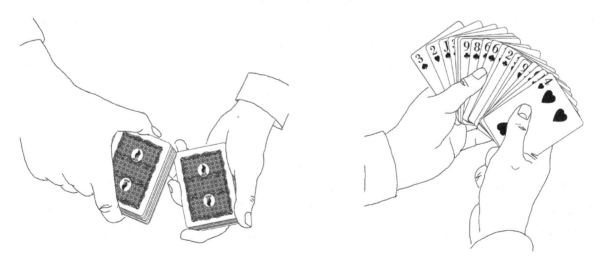

The Lady with X-ray Vision

This self-working trick will add variety to your card magic routine. As a blind magician, the storyline works great for me. I am sure you will enjoy performing this trick as much as your audience enjoys watching it!

Effect: The magician tells the story of the Lady with X-ray Vision. Then he asks a spectator to shuffle a deck of cards (you can use any deck of cards). The magician takes the deck of cards to get to the Lady with X-ray Vision. He pulls out the Queen of Hearts. He then asks the spectator to cut the cards. The magician takes half the deck and places it aside. He then makes three stacks of cards with the other portion of cards. He then asks the spectator to hide the top three cards in his pocket or behind his back. The magician calls attention to the Lady with X-ray Vision, which is the Queen of Hearts. He picks up the Queen and has her "scan" the spectator. He has a "conversation" with the Queen. The magician, along with help from the Lady with X-ray Vision, reveals the spectator's three cards!

Setup: No setup is required for this trick. It can be done with a borrowed, shuffled deck.

Performance: Ask a spectator to thoroughly shuffle the cards. Take the cards from the spectator and say, *"I would like to introduce you to a very special lady. She has special magical powers. Here she is."* While going through the deck looking for the Queen of Hearts, look at the first three cards that are on top of the deck (see illustration). Of course, if you turn the deck face down, these cards would be on the bottom of the deck. Memorize the three cards. For now, just remember the number or whether it is a Jack, Queen or King. Later, when you are really comfortable doing this trick you can remember the value and the suit of the card.

For instructional purposes, let's say the top three cards are the Three of Clubs, the Six of Hearts and the Eight of Diamonds. All you have to remember is 3-6-8. (It is easy to remember the cards like this. Even if there is a face card, it is still easy. For example, if the cards were King of Clubs, Two of Spades and Jack of Diamonds, just remember K-2-J.)

Take the Queen of Hearts and prop her up against the upright card case. Say, *"It is important for the Lady to observe all the activity."* Set the rest of the deck down on the table. Say to the spectator, *"Please pick up the deck of cards."*

"Good. I would now like you to deal out the cards in three separate stacks. Do this until all the cards have been dealt. Okay. Now take the top card off of each pile and hide them in your pocket, or you can place them behind your back."

Pick up the Queen of Hearts and say, *"I told you earlier that the Queen of Hearts has special magical powers. In fact, she is called the Lady with X-ray Vision. There is only one way to prove this to you. Watch closely."*

Take the Queen and move it back and forth, as if you were scanning the spectator. Move it especially slow past the spectator's pocket (or level with the area where the spectator put his three cards).

Now take the Queen and hold it up to your ear. Act as though you are listening to what the Queen is "telling" you. Say, *"The Lady says that your cards are ... a two ... a six ... and an eight."* Ask the spectator to show his cards to show that they match the revelation of the Lady with X-ray Vision.

The illustration below shows how to look at the three cards that are on top of the face up deck. Look at these cards naturally, while you are looking for the Queen of Hearts.

Magic Almanac

This easy to do trick is self-working and requires no sleight of hand. It uses the Key Card Principle.

Effect: A spectator selects a card and returns it to the deck. The magician then uses the deck as an almanac to reveal the spectator's chosen card.

Setup: Reverse the bottom card on the deck.

Performance: Before you perform the trick, reverse the bottom card on the deck. In other words, turn the bottom card face up.

Spread the cards between your hands so the spectator can select a card. (Be careful not to expose the bottom card, which is face up). Say to the spectator, *"Please select a card. Look at it and remember it, but do not tell me what it is."* For instructional purposes, let's assume the spectator chose the King of Diamonds.

Square up the deck and say, *"Please place your card on top of the deck. Good. Now please cut the deck and complete the cut."* (By doing this, the Key Card which is the reversed card—is now directly on top of the spectator's chosen card.)

Say to the spectator, *"Isn't it true that your chosen card is now lost somewhere in the deck?"* The spectator will agree. Ribbon Spread the cards on the table. Act as surprised as the spectator when you see the reversed card. (As a blind magician, I ask the spectator if he sees anything unusual in the cards. He will tell me that one card is face up. I ask him to show me with his finger where it is. That's how I know where to cut the cards and where the Key Card is.).

Say, *"Wow! That's unusual. I think that card is telling us where we should cut the deck. Let's do it."* Cut the cards so that the Key Card is now on top of the deck. In other words, take all the cards that were on top of the reversed card, and put them on the bottom of the deck. Square up the deck, and place the cards on the table.

Turn over the face up card, which is now on top of the deck. (Only you will know that the spectator's chosen card is now directly under the top card.)

Say to the spectator and audience, *"Almost everyone has heard of the Farmers' Almanac. It contains information on just about everything. What some people don't know is that we can use a deck of cards in the same way. Please let me demonstrate."*

Say to the spectator, *"How many weeks are there in a year?"* The spectator will reply fifty-two. Say, *"Good. Okay, fifty-two. That's a five and a two. Deal off five cards, one at a time, from the top of the deck. Count them out and make a small pile of cards on the table."* The spectator will count out five cards. Then say, *"Good. Now count out two cards and place them in a small pile."*

Point at each pile and say, *"Five and two."* Pick up the pile of two cards and place them on top of the pile of five cards. Now place this packet of cards on top of the deck.

Say to the spectator, *"How many months are there in a year?"* The spectator will answer twelve. Say, *"Good. Count out twelve cards on the table. Please count them out loud."* The spectator will deal out twelve cards on the table. Say, *"Okay, now pick up the twelve cards and place them on top of the deck."*

Ask the spectator, *"How many days in a week?"* The spectator will answer seven. Say, *"Good. Deal out seven cards on the table."* The spectator will count out seven cards. Say, *"Okay, put those cards on top of the deck."* Now ask the spectator, *"What time is it?"* Before he can answer, say, *"Just kidding. It's time to find your card."*

Ask the spectator, *"What was the name of your card? It's okay for you to tell me."* In our example, the spectator chose the King of Diamonds. *"Remember I said that the Farmers' Almanac had information on just about everything you would want to know? So does a deck of cards. As you are aware, the cards have been thoroughly mixed up from all the dealing as I asked you questions. However, if you take the top card and turn it over ... you will find your card."* Have the spectator turn over the top card. It will be his chosen card!

Face Up & Face Down

This is a great opener for a card routine. It is very visual and will make an impact on your audience.

Effect: The magician shows a deck of cards. He first riffles the cards to show that all the face cards are thoroughly mixed up and in a random order. He then riffles the cards to show that all the backs are as they should be. Then, with a snap of the fingers, the magician spreads the cards on the table. Magically, there is now a face up card sandwiched in between every face down card. It is visually stunning!

Setup: This is one of the few tricks in this book that requires setting up the deck before you perform, but it is well worth the time it takes because it has such a visual impact on the audience. I would suggest using this trick as an opener, which means it should be done as the first trick in your routine. You can then use the deck for other card tricks. If you prefer to do this trick later in your routine, you can simply switch decks from the one used for other card tricks to this one that's been set up.

To set up the deck, simply turn half the deck over so half is face up and half is face down. Now mesh the cards together using the Riffle Shuffle so that a face up card falls in between each face down card. With practice, you will be able to do this very easily. You can also do this by pushing the cards together so they intermesh with the face up cards in between every face down card. If you prefer, you may take a face down card and lay a face up card on top. Continue to do this one card at a time. However, it is important to leave *ALL* the face up cards jogged out of the deck about a quarter-inch. This is what enables you to show the cards as a normal deck of cards. I wrap the cards with a rubber band to hold them in place until I begin the trick.

Performance: Say to the audience, *"I would like to show you that all the cards have been thoroughly mixed up."* Riffle the stack of face up cards to show that all the cards are face up. This is done by placing your thumb over the top of the deck and riffling the cards. Now do the same thing with the stack of cards that are face down. Say, *"And of course the backs are as they should be."* Turn the deck, and riffle the cards with your thumb to show that all the backs of the cards are in order.

Say, *"Please watch as the magic takes place."* Snap your fingers and Ribbon Spread the cards on the table. A face up card is now sandwiched in between every face down card! Your audience might think you are using a trick deck of cards, such as a Svengali deck, so they really will be impressed when you immediately use the cards in another effect in which you have a spectator shuffle the cards.

The Outta Sight Prediction Trick

This trick will add some variety to your card routine. It uses a great method to force a card. You can use this force for other card tricks. As a blind magician, this trick works well in my card routine.

Effect: The magician places a deck of cards under a handkerchief. He asks a spectator to cut the cards at any place he chooses. The magician picks up the bottom portion of the cards and asks the spectator to look at the top card of this portion. The magician then asks the spectator to look inside the card case, which has been sitting on the table since the beginning of the trick. Inside the box is a folded-up piece of paper. The spectator unfolds the paper and reads it aloud. It correctly predicts the spectator's chosen card!

Setup: You will need a handkerchief for this trick. It is important that the cards cannot be seen while under the handkerchief, so make sure the fabric is not too thin. On a small piece of paper, write "YOU WILL SELECT THE — (write the name of the "force" card)." Fold up the piece of paper, and place it in the bottom of the card case. Find the card that you wrote on the paper, and place it on the top of the deck. For example, if you wrote "YOU WILL SELECT THE QUEEN OF HEARTS," put the Queen of Hearts on top of the deck.

Performance: Take the deck of cards out of the card case. Set the card case down on the table. Hold the deck, face down, in your right hand. Put the handkerchief over the cards. As soon as you cover the cards, turn the deck face up. Do this without calling any attention to it. (Practice this move so you can do it smoothly and without making any motion with your arm. The audience will assume the deck is face down).

Drape the handkerchief over the cards. Say to the spectator, *"Please cut the cards. Cut them anywhere you like. It is important that you have a free choice and that I am not influencing you in any way."* As the spectator lifts off the upper portion of cards, turn the bottom half over so they are face down. (The top card will be the force card you placed there before the trick). Say to the spectator, *"Please take the top card. Look at it and show it to the audience, but don't tell me what it is. Keep the card and place it face down on the table."* As he shows the card to the audience, take the cards and place them under the handkerchief. Without calling any attention to it, turn the cards over and place them against the other cards. (At this point the deck is under the handkerchief and are all face up.)

Turn the deck face down as you remove the handkerchief. Do not let the audience see the cards until you have turned them face down. Practice this move until you can do it all with one smooth move. Place the deck of cards and the handkerchief on the table.

Now say, *"You have the card you selected. I would now like you to open the card case. Remember that the card case has been sitting on the table since the beginning of the trick."*

Let the spectator open the card case. He will see the folded-up paper. When he removes it from the case, say, *"Please unfold the paper and read aloud what is written on it."* He will read the words on the paper, which will indicate his chosen card.

Jack-in-the-Box

This is a very easy to do prediction trick, but it has a powerful impact on the audience.

Effect: The magician fans through the cards and selects a card. He says it is a "prediction." He places the card in the card case. The magician then asks a spectator to select a card. The magician says that his prediction card will be the same color and denomination as the spectator's card, but of a different suit. He asks the spectator to open the card case and show the audience the prediction card. Amazingly, it is the same color and denomination as the spectator's chosen card.

Setup: Put the Jack of Hearts on the bottom of the deck before you perform the trick.

Performance: Say to the audience, *"I would like to go through the deck and pick a card that will be my prediction card."* Take out the Jack of Diamonds. Do not show it to the audience. Say, *"I will place it into the card case for safekeeping. I will place the card case in full view during the trick."* Put the Jack of Diamonds in the card case.

Now select a spectator from the audience. Say, *"I would now like you to say stop at any time."* Put the deck of cards in your left hand. As you do this, push the bottom card (the Jack of Hearts) toward you about a half-inch. (The deck will hide the jogged card). Put your right hand on top of the deck. Use your right middle finger to push back the cards. Push back on the tops of the cards, about an inch and a half, one card at a time until the spectator says *"Stop."*

When the spectator says stop, pull off the pulled-back portion of cards. And as you are doing this, slide the bottom card back, along with the top portion of cards. Do this by putting your right thumb on top of the top portion, with your right index finger on the bottom card. Pull the cards back together, and then in one motion, show the spectator the bottom card (the Jack of Hearts). This is a variation of a "slide force." It is easy to do and is used by many card magicians.

Say, *"This is where you stopped me."* Show the bottom card and say, *"Please take it."* Hand the spectator the bottom card of the pulled-off portion (you know it is the Jack of Hearts). *"Remember, I said my prediction would be of the same color and same denomination but a different suit than your chosen card. Would you please open up the card case and show everyone what my prediction was."*

The spectator will open up the card case and show everyone the Jack of Diamonds!

The *Amazing* Spectator

This is one of my favorite tricks. You will find it easy to learn and perform. Tricks that involve audience participation are fun to do for both you and the audience.

Effect: In this trick, the spectator locates his previously selected card. I usually do this trick after showing a few card tricks and then tell a spectator that I'd like him to do a trick. I usually call the spectator the "Amazing" someone—I say the person's name. For example, the Amazing John. I will sometimes add "dini" to whatever his name is. For example, the Amazing Johndini. The audience finds this amusing, and it is a good way to get started with the trick.

Setup: No setup is required.

Presentation: Say to the spectator, *"I would like you to do the magic this time. Please shuffle the cards."* After the spectator shuffles the cards, say, *"Please place the cards on the palm of my left hand. Now, cut the cards about halfway. You take about half the cards, and leave me with about half. I'll put the cards behind my back so I can't see them."* (Because I am blind, the audience always thinks it's funny when I say this.)

Tell the spectator, *"Go through your cards and make a free selection of any card. Show the card to the audience, but don't tell me what it is, and don't show it to me."* (Once again, the audience finds it amusing that I would tell the spectator not to show me the card.)

Tell the spectator, *"Now place your selected card on top of your packet of cards, and hold the cards face down on your palm."* While the spectator is doing this, you do the following with the cards that are behind your back: Reverse the bottom card so that it is now face up. Then reverse the second card from the top of your packet so that it is face up.

Now bring your packet of cards around in front of you, and place them on top of the spectator's packet. By doing this, you have secretly put a reversed card above the spectator's chosen card.

Now say, *"Please take the deck of cards and put it behind your back. Take the top card off and place it on the bottom of the deck. Now take the next card and turn it face up, and place it in the middle of the deck."*

Now for the big finish. Tell the spectator to bring the cards around in front of him. Say, *"The Amazing Johndini (or whatever the spectator's name is) will now perform one of magic's greatest tricks. Please tap the deck of cards with your finger."* This is to dramatically build up the effect. *"Now snap your fingers over the deck."* Once again, this is done only to build up the presentation of the trick. *"Now thumb through the cards until you come to the card you reversed in the deck."*

Once the spectator comes to the reversed card, say, *"Good! What was the card you selected?"*

After the spectator names his card, say, *"Look at the card under the face up card."* When the spectator turns the card over, it will be his chosen card. Say, *"Ladies and Gentlemen, give a nice round of applause for the Amazing Johndini."*

When you put your packet of cards on top of the spectator's packet of cards, you will be secretly putting the reversed card above the spectator's chosen card. Once the cards are in a Ribbon Spread, the reversed card will appear as the only face up card. When you tell the spectator to look at the card under the face up card, it will be his chosen card. In the illustration above, the Queen of Hearts is the reversed card, and the Four of Hearts is the spectator's chosen card.

The Magic of Three

You will be able to learn this trick in a matter of minutes.

Effect: The magician tells the audience that there is magic in the number three. He then takes any number 3 card out of the deck. He turns it face up and replaces it in the deck. He fans the cards to show that the 3 is the only face up card in the deck. He asks a spectator to select a card and replace it in the deck. The cards are cut once—twice, if the spectator wishes to do so. The magician goes through the deck again to show the face up 3 card. He once again claims that the number three has magical powers and uses it for a "magic wand." He counts down three cards. The magician asks the spectator which card he selected. The magician turns over the third card, and it is the spectator's chosen card.

Setup: No setup is required for this trick.

Performance: Ask a spectator to shuffle a deck of cards. Say, *"It is believed by many that the number three has special magical powers. I think this trick will prove it."* Take the cards and openly find any number 3 card. Turn the card face up, and put it somewhere in the upper one-third of the deck.

Fan out the cards to show the spectator that the 3 card is indeed the only face up card in the deck. When you come to the number 3 card, show it to the spectator and say, *"As you can see, the three is the only face up card in the deck."* At this time, push two other cards under the 3 card. Do this casually and without calling any attention to it. Just push the two cards under the 3 card with your fingers that are under the deck. Keep this portion of the cards a little separated from the rest of the deck. Without hesitating, keep thumbing the rest of the cards to the right.

Ask the spectator, *"Would you please select a card?"* Have the spectator select a card from the portion of cards that are under the number 3 card (and the two cards that are under the 3 card).

Say, *"Please remember your card and show it to the audience, but don't tell me what it is. If you are not happy with that card, you may choose another one. I want you to be happy with your choice."*

Now put the portion of cards that you have in your right hand on the bottom of the deck. (Only you know that the face up number 3 card is now the third card up from the bottom).

Shuffle the deck with the Overhand Shuffle. This is a false shuffle because you do not disturb the order of the bottom three cards. In other words, the bottom three cards will always stay at the bottom of the deck and will always be in your right hand. To do this, pick up about two-thirds of the bottom of the deck with your right hand. Now let a few cards drop in front of the portion of cards in your left hand. Do this motion over and over, but remember not to disturb the order of the bottom three cards in your right hand.

Ask the spectator to tell you when to stop shuffling. When he does, ask him to put his chosen card on top of the cards in your left hand. Then put the cards that are in your right hand on top of the cards in your left hand. (By doing this, you have put the face up number 3 card in the position of three cards above the spectator's chosen card.)

Ask the spectator to cut the cards—I always then ask if he would like to make a second cut. I think this adds to the performance of the trick.

Say, *"When we first began the trick, I told you that the number three has always had magical powers. Let's see what happens."*

Fan through the deck until you come to the face up 3 card. Say, *"There it is. Please watch closely."* Take the cards that are on top of the face up number 3 card and set them to one side. Pick up the 3 card and use it like a magic wand, making a few passes over the deck of cards. Then tap the top of the deck with the 3 card. Say, *"That should do it."*

Ask the spectator, *"What was your card?"*

Set the face up 3 card to the side. Now slowly count, *"One, two, three."* Slowly turn over the card. It will be the spectator's chosen card!

The Magic of Three

This illustration shows how to spread the cards to show the spectator that the 3 card is the only face up card in the deck. As you do this, push two other cards under the 3 card. Do this casually and naturally. Just use your fingers that are under the deck to pull the other two cards underneath the 3 card. Keep this portion of cards separated a little from the rest of the deck.

Cardiac Card

This trick has been around for a long time and is in many card magic books. It is easy to do and is fun for the audience.

Effect: A spectator thoroughly shuffles a deck of cards. Then he selects a card from the deck. He cuts the cards. The magician then uses the spectator's heartbeat to find the spectator's chosen card!

Setup: No setup is required for this trick.

Performance: Ask a spectator to thoroughly shuffle the cards. When he gives the cards back to you, turn the deck slightly and look at the bottom card. This is the Key Card. Let's assume the bottom card is a Three of Hearts.

Fan the cards out. Say to the spectator, *"Please select a card. Remember it and show it to the audience, but don't tell me what it is."* (Before he looks at the card, I always ask if he would like to select another card. I think this adds to the performance). Let's say he chose the Queen of Hearts.

Say, *"Now I am going to put five stacks of cards on the table."* (The magician now puts five stacks of cards on the table using all the cards he has in his hands). To do this take approximately ten cards and place the stack down on the table. Put another stack of about ten cards next to the first stack. Do this three more times until all the cards are on the table in five stacks of cards. Say, *"I would now like you to put your card on top of any stack of cards that are on the table."*

Now place the last stack of cards (the one with the Key Card on the bottom) on top of the spectators chosen stack. When you do this it will put the Key Card on top of the spectators chosen card. Now put the other three stacks of cards on top of this stack. You will now have an entire deck of cards on the table.

Say, *"Good, now of course, at this point neither one of us knows where your card is located in the deck, but I am going to try to find your card. I will need your help."*

Turn the deck face up and spread the cards out on the table so that most of the faces show. As you spread them, look for the Key Card in this example, the Three of Hearts. You will then know that the card directly to the right of the Key Card is the spectator's chosen card. (This is if you have spread the cards from left to right.) Do not call attention to the chosen card yet.

Say, *"We all know that a person's heart rate increases when he becomes excited. Your pulse rate will speed up when you see your card. So I will use your own heart rate to tell me where your card is."*

Take the spectator's wrist in your hand. Say, *"Yes, I can feel your pulse. I now want you to point your index finger."* Move the spectator's hand over the cards. Bend his wrist so that his index finger is over the cards. Start at one end of the cards, and move from card to card. Say, *"Hm-m-m ... nothing yet."*

As you get closer to the spectator's card, say, *"Wow, your heart rate is really picking up. Do you see your card?"* The spectator will answer yes.

When you come to the spectator's card (the Queen of Hearts), push his finger on it. *"Your pulse is racing, so this must be your card."* Pick up the Queen of Hearts and show it to your audience. Say, *"That worked out great. Maybe I should have been a ... cardiologist!"*

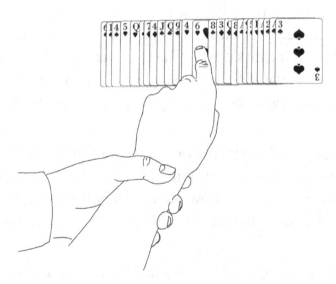

This illustration shows you how the magician holds the spectators wrist. The magician then pushes the spectator's finger over the chosen card. In this illustration the spectators chosen card is the Six of Hearts.

Doc Does It Again

This easy to learn card trick will add some variety to your card magic routine. It requires no sleight of hand and no complicated moves. Your audience will love this entertaining story—and of course, the surprise ending!

Effect: The magician tells a story about the famous gambler, Doc Holiday. He demonstrates how Doc would stack the cards so that he would have four Aces in his hand. On one occasion, Doc stacked the deck and dealt out four hands of cards. It came down to a hand of cards between Doc and another gambler. The other person knew that Doc had stacked the deck, so he said he would make a bet if he could have Doc's hand of cards instead of his own. Doc accepted. The spectator thought that he had the winning hand, but when he turned the cards over, he didn't have anything. Of course, Doc Holiday turned over his cards to reveal he had four Aces!

Setup: There is no setup required for this trick. It may be done with a borrowed deck.

Performance: Say to the audience, *"I am sure that most of you have heard of the famous Doc Holiday. He is probably best known for his part in the shootout at the OK Corral, but Doc was also quite the gambler. There were many people who thought that Doc cheated at cards. Sometimes he would show them how he stacked the deck with Aces."*

Openly take the deck of cards (it can be a borrowed deck that has been thoroughly shuffled) and take out the four Aces. Place them face up in a row on the table.

Count out ten cards from the remainder of the deck. Do this by pushing them to the right with your left thumb. Count in small groups of two and three until you get to ten. Do this silently and do not call attention to the number of cards you have counted out. Set the rest of the deck down on the table, and put the ten cards in your left hand.

Now say, " *Doc Holiday would actually show how he stacked the deck before a game of cards. He would put three cards on top of each of the Aces. Here's how he did it.*"

Turn one of the Aces face down—it doesn't matter which one. Count out three cards from the packet, one at a time, and place them on the Ace. Count out loud, *"One, two, and three."* Then place the remainder of the packet on top of the dealt-out cards and pick up the entire packet.

Do this same thing to another of the Aces. Turn one of the Aces face down, and count out three cards, one at a time, and put them on top of the Ace. Once again, place the remainder of the packet on top of the dealt-out cards, and pick up the entire packet.

Do the same thing for the other two face up Aces that are on the table. Pick up the entire packet and place it in your left hand.

Tell your audience, *"Doc would then say, 'And here's how I stack the cards. I put four cards on the bottom of the packet.'"* Do just that. While counting aloud, take four cards, one at a time, and move them from the top to the bottom. Count *"One, two, three and four."*

Take the small packet of cards and place on top of the rest of the deck.

Say, *"Doc would say that is how he stacked the cards to deal himself the four Aces. He would demonstrate this by saying he would deal out four poker hands to four different people."* Deal out five cards to four positions, as if you were dealing cards to four people. Now say, *"After the cards were dealt, Doc would say, 'Let's see what the first person has.'"* Turn up the cards that were dealt to the *first* person. *"Doc would say to that first person, 'There isn't much use for you to stay in the game, especially when you know I have four Aces.' Then he'd say, 'Let's see what the third person has.'"* Turn up the cards that were dealt to the *third* person. *"Not much here either. Then Doc would ask the second player, 'Who do you think has the best hand?'* Of course, the second person would say that Doc had the best hand. Doc would say, *'What if I were to give you one of my Aces? You would now have six cards and a good chance to win.'"*

Take one of the cards in "Doc's" hand and put it under the *second* person's cards. "Doc would ask the second person if he would like to bet on his hand. Of course, the other gambler would say no—he knew that Doc still had the other three Aces. Doc then would say, *'How would you bet if we were to switch cards?'* The other gambler couldn't believe it and would say, *'I'd bet all the money on the table!'* And with that, Doc would push his cards over to the other gambler and take the gambler's cards. *The other gambler would turn over his cards, expecting to see a great winning hand—but he didn't have one. There were no Aces in his hand. Doc would smile and turn over his hand of cards.*" Turn over the cards that are Doc's. There will be the four Aces! Say, "*Doc did it again!*"

The Magical Happy Birthday Trick

This is a unique trick that can be used for just about any special occasion. It will add variety to your card routine.

Effect: The magician (that's you) asks the audience if anyone has recently had a birthday. He shuffles the deck and asks the birthday person to select a card. The card is returned to the deck. The magician then asks another spectator to sing "Happy Birthday" to the birthday person. As the second spectator sings, he deals off a card for every word he sings in the birthday song. The magician stops the second spectator from dealing on the last word of the song. The magician then asks the birthday person which card he selected. The second spectator turns over the card he is holding—it is the birthday person's selected card!

Setup: There is no setup required for this trick. It can be done with a borrowed, shuffled deck.

Performance: Shuffle the cards. With the backs of the cards toward you, spread the cards between your hands. Thumb over the cards from left to right. Count out fifteen cards, but do this without alerting the audience that you are counting the cards. Count to fifteen in small groups of three or four cards. Keep the fifteen cards slightly separated from the rest of the deck. While you are doing this, say, *"Is there anyone in our audience who has recently had a birthday or who has a birthday coming up?"* In all my years of doing this trick, someone has always answered yes when I ask this. If no one responds, ask if anyone will have a birthday within a month, two months, etc., until someone responds.

Say to the birthday person, *"Good. I would like you to select a card. Do not tell me what it is, but remember which card you selected."* Let him choose from the cards that are in the lower portion of the deck. (Not from the stack of fifteen cards.)

Say, *"Now place the card near the center of the deck."* Hold the lower portion out toward the spectator so he can place his selected card on top of the lower portion. Place the fifteen cards in your right hand on top of the chosen card and square up the deck.

Now select another spectator. Say, *"I would like you to sing 'Happy Birthday' to our birthday person. And as you sing each word of the song, deal off a card and place it on the table."*

As the second spectator sings, make sure he puts a card on the table for each word. When he gets to the last word of the song, say *"stop."* The second spectator will be left holding one card. Ask the birthday person, *"What was your selected card?"*

Tell the second spectator to turn over the card he is holding. It will be the birthday person's chosen card!

Note: This trick can be adapted to almost any special occasion, such as a wedding, graduation, promotion, etc. Just adapt the song so it has sixteen words or sixteen beats. The sixteenth card will always be the chosen card!

Ace Through the Deck

This is a quick and easy to do trick. It is very simple yet makes your audience think of you as a master of sleight of hand.

Effect: The magician shows three cards—the Ace of Diamonds, the Two of Diamonds, and the Three of Diamonds. He places these cards on top of the deck. He slaps the top of the deck and magically, the Ace of Diamonds has "jumped" to the bottom of the deck!

Setup: Cover the Ace of Hearts in a V-shape pattern with the Two of Diamonds and the Three of Diamonds. Cover the Ace of Hearts so that it appears to be the Ace of Diamonds. Make sure you cover the Heart in the corner index on the Ace of Hearts.

Performance: Say to the audience, *"I have three cards—the Ace of Diamonds, the Two of Diamonds, and the Three of Diamonds."* Show the three cards as described in the setup. Square them up and place them on top of the deck.

Tell the audience to watch very closely, and then slap the top of the deck. Say, *"Magically, the Ace of Diamonds has gone through the deck and is now on the bottom."* Show the Ace of Diamonds on the bottom of the deck.

In a natural manner, immediately shuffle the deck. I do this because someone might remark that you simply used two Ace of Diamonds and had one on top and one on the bottom. If this happens just say, *"That would make it easy, but then I couldn't let you inspect the cards—like this."* Then hand the person the deck of cards, and he will see there is only one Ace of Diamonds.

Ace Through the Deck

This illustration shows how the Three of Diamonds and the Two of Diamonds are placed over the Ace of Hearts to make it look like an Ace of Diamonds.

A Roll of the Dice

This is a classic prediction trick. As a blind magician, I like tricks that are self-working and easy to do. As you will see, you do not need vision to perform this trick. This trick is found in most beginning card magic books. One of the best explanations of this trick was given by Criss Angel on his *Mindfreak* TV show.

Effect: The magician shows the spectator a sealed envelope that is marked PREDICTION. He then asks the spectator to roll dice. The spectator is given the opportunity to roll the dice as many times as he wishes. When he is satisfied, the magician asks the spectator to add the two numbers on the top of the dice with the two numbers on the bottom of the dice. The spectator takes a deck of cards and counts out the cards to the number that was the sum total of the numbers on the dice. The card positioned at the dice total number is shown to the audience. The spectator is asked to open a sealed envelope. The card inside matches the spectator's chosen card!

Setup: To perform this trick you need to know which card is fourteenth from the top of the deck. Then take a duplicate (from another deck) of the card that is fourteenth from the top of the deck, and place it in a sealed envelope.

Note: An alternative to using a duplicate card is to simply write on a piece of paper what your prediction is, and seal it in the envelope.

You will also need a pair of dice. The dice can be borrowed, and in fact, this makes for an even better effect, as it removes all doubt over whether the dice are loaded or gimmicked. The secret to the trick is this: No matter how the dice are rolled, the sum of the top and bottom numbers will always be fourteen! Try it, and you will see how it works.

Performance: Set the sealed envelope and the deck of cards on the table. Point to the envelope and say, *"Inside this envelope is my prediction."*

Hand the spectator the dice and say, *"I would like for you to roll the dice to come up with a random number. You may roll the dice one at a time or both together. It is your choice. You may also roll the dice as many times as you want."* Once the spectator is satisfied with the roll of the dice, say, *"Now add the two numbers that are on top of the dice. Good. Now turn the dice over and add the two numbers on the bottom of the dice. Good. Now please add those two sums together."*

No matter how the spectator rolled the dice, the total will be fourteen. Say, *"Now count down to the fourteenth card in the deck, and show it to the audience."* After the spectator does this, say, *"Please open the sealed envelope, which has been in full view since we started the trick."*

The spectator will open the envelope, and it will match the selected card.

Money
Magic

The Magic of Money!

Magic performed with money is another popular type of magic. Just as there are magicians who specialize in card magic, there are also magicians who perform exclusively with coins and bills. One of the great things about money magic is that you always have the props available. Almost everyone carries some coins or bills.

Many tricks with money do not require any advanced sleight of hand or complicated techniques. It is my intention to provide you only with tricks that are easy to learn. If you wish to learn advanced coin magic, many resources are available. J. B. Bobo's book *Modern Coin Magic* is a great source. If you prefer to learn from watching video, I suggest any video by David Roth, one of the finest coin magicians in the country. There are also several books and videos on coin magic for beginners. If you are interested in performing money magic, I strongly recommend that you contact a local magic store to see about taking magic classes. This is how I learned to do the coin magic I perform in my close-up magic routine.

Coin magic can add variety to a close-up magic routine. I usually do a coin trick, followed by two or three card tricks. Then I do another coin trick. Three of my favorite coin tricks are Scotch & Soda, Matrix, and a three-coin transposition. In Scotch & Soda, a centavo and a half-dollar are placed into a spectator's hand. The spectator closes his hand and in the end, the centavo changes into a quarter.

Matrix is a coin-assembly routine in which coins disappear from under a card and reappear under a different card. The three-coin transposition begins with a centavo, a Chinese coin, and a half-dollar. The coins vanish from one hand and reappear in the other. There are, of course, hundreds of different coin and bill tricks. It seems the audience really enjoys coin and bill magic. I suppose this is because coins and bills are easy to relate to, as most people handle them on a daily basis.

I learned my first coin routine by taking magic classes at a local magic shop. I also learned many coin routines from my magician friends. This is a great way to learn new moves and variations on routines. I also have several books and videos that deal specifically with money magic.

Once again, I have tried to cite the proper source for the tricks. I feel it is very important to acknowledge the creator or inventor of a trick or method, whenever possible.

Conjuring with Coins

The tricks in this section can be done easily and with minimal preparation. If you enjoy doing coin tricks then I feel I should let you know that some "money miracles" can be accomplished with the use of gimmicked coins. Some of the classic coin tricks are achieved using specialized coins such as a shell (a coin that covers another coin), a magnetized coin or a folding coin.

There are also several props that are made just for coin magic. The Okito Coin Box is a great prop to use in the transposition, production or vanishing of a coin. A Coin Drawer Box can make a coin vanish and then reappear. Some magic manufacturers such as Johnson Magic and Sterling Magic specialize in making high quality coin effects.

So, if after reading this book you want to do more advanced coin magic, I would suggest visiting a magic store and asking them to demonstrate a simple coin trick. I would also recommend J.B. Bobo's book, *Modern Coin Magic*. This book is one of the best resources for learning coin magic. If you really want to sharpen your skills with coin magic I would recommend any video by coin magic experts such as Dean Dill or David Roth. They can help you to take your coin conjuring to a very advanced level.

While it is important to practice all magic often, this is especially true of coin magic. A coin sleight or move that is not done properly may cause "flashing" (exposing the coin) or "talking" (the sound of two coins hitting each other) when they should not be doing so. You should practice the moves until you can perform the trick smoothly and in a natural, relaxed manner. The more you practice the more you will gain confidence in your performance.

I love money magic and hope you will like it too. Some of my favorite effects to perform with coins are Scotch & Soda, Coin Transposition, Matrix and Miser's Dream.

Scotch & Soda is a coin trick in which a centavo (a Mexican coin) changes into a quarter. This is one of the most popular of all coin tricks. It is the first coin trick that I learned when I started doing magic. There are many versions of the Coin

Transposition trick. In my routine, I use a Kennedy half dollar, a centavo and a Chinese coin. In the routine the half dollar changes places with the centavo and Chinese coin. It is a very stunning effect. At the end of the trick all the coins can be examined by the audience. Matrix is a coin assembly routine in which four coins are placed under four playing cards. Amazingly, all four coins wind up under one of the playing cards! Matrix requires some coin sleights but it is well worth the practice time to perform this great trick. Miser's Dream is a coin production routine. I do Miser's Dream with music in my stage magic routine.

Flash Cash

My good friend Joshua Jay contributed this trick. Joshua Jay is one of the finest magicians in the world. He has traveled to many different countries, performing and conducting lectures on magic. He is a fantastic author and is the creator of many fine magic effects.
As a blind magician, I love this particular trick because it does not require sight to perform. It is easy to do, and I am sure your audience will love it!

Effect: The magician talks about taking a trip to Las Vegas. He explains how a fake bank roll is sometimes used to impress people so that they might invite you to play in a high-stakes poker game. The magician shows the audience how to make the fake bank roll out of blank pieces of paper. Of course, everyone knows you need *REAL* money to play in Vegas. Fortunately, the magician uses a snap of the fingers to turn the fake bank roll into real money!

Setup: You need to make two different bank rolls. The first is made of real money. Take about twenty one-dollar bills and roll them up. Wrap a rubber band around the roll, and let it set for a couple of days. This will help to hold the bills together when the rubber band is taken off.

Now make the fake bank roll. To do this, trace around a dollar bill on a piece of blank computer paper. Make twenty of these blank pieces of paper. Cut them out and roll them together, just like the real bank roll. Put a rubber band around this roll also, and let it set for a couple of days. This will ensure that the fake bank roll is similar in appearance to the real bank roll.

Put the real bank roll (without a rubber band around it) in your *left* pocket. (It is best to do this trick with pockets that have easy access. A jacket pocket is best, but large, loose pants pockets will work also.) Put a dollar bill and a rubber band in the *right* pocket. Put the roll of blank paper (without a rubber band around it) next to the real money roll in your *left* pocket.

Performance: Say to the audience, *"I once took a trip to Las Vegas. I didn't have any money, but I made a flash roll. Let me show you how I did it. I took a roll of blank pieces of paper, and I simply wrapped a real bill around it."* Reach into your left pocket and remove the roll of blank pieces of paper. Then reach into your right pocket and remove the dollar bill. Wrap the dollar bill around the paper roll.

Say, *"I used this flash cash to act like I had a lot of money, hoping that someone would invite me to a high-stakes poker game."*

(Note: This is a great setup for the next trick in my close-up routine, called Ace in the Hole, in which a worthless poker hand is turned into four Aces!)

"Of course, I had to make sure that nobody saw the blank pieces of paper in my flash cash, so I held it tightly with a rubber band." Put the paper roll in your left hand. Now put your left hand into the left pocket. Leave the paper roll there, but switch it for the real money roll. At the same time you put your left hand in the left pocket, put your right hand in your right pocket to get the rubber band. THIS IS IMPORTANT: Pull out your right hand a split-second before you pull out your left hand (with the real money roll). This action will look as though you are merely going through both pockets in search of a rubber band.

Wrap the rubber band around the real money roll. (The audience will assume you are wrapping the rubber band around the fake paper roll.)

Say, *"Of course, I am sure you are wondering what I used for money when I got into the poker game. Well, in that case, it's a good thing I'm a magician. I just snapped my fingers and turned the flash cash into real money!"* Take off the rubber band and show the audience the roll of real money!

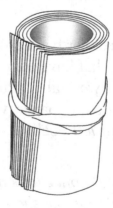

This illustration shows you how to wrap the roll of paper bills with a rubber band. Then make an identical roll with real money.

Turnover Coin Vanish

This is a quick and easy coin vanishing trick. It takes a little practice, but it is well worth the effort.

Effect: The magician holds a coin in the palm of each hand. He turns his hands over and places them on the table. Magically, the coin in the right hand has disappeared. The left hand is lifted to show that the coin that disappeared from the right hand is now with the coin in the left hand.

Setup: There is no setup required for this trick. It may be done with borrowed coins.

Performance: Borrow two coins of the same denomination from someone in the audience. I prefer to use quarters, but it can be done with any two coins. Place one coin in each of your upturned palms. It is important where you place the coins.

The coin in the left hand should be placed just below where the little finger and the ring finger come together. Place the coin about a quarter-inch below this junction. The coin in the right hand should be placed just below (about a quarter-inch) where the right thumb connects to the rest of the hand.

Say to the audience, *"One coin in each hand. Please watch."* Hold your hands about a foot (twelve inches) apart and about two inches above the table.

Now very quickly (and at the same time), turn your hands over and down on the table. Bring the hands down so that the thumbs are almost touching (no more than an inch apart). By doing this, the coin that is in the right hand will be thrown under the left hand. Practice this move repeatedly until you can do it very smoothly.

Say, *"As you can see, the coin under this hand has vanished."* Lift up your right hand to show that the coin is gone. With your right hand snap your fingers over your left hand. Say, *"And there it is!"* Lift up your left hand to show that both coins are now together.

Turnover Coin Vanish

The illustration on the left shows where to place the coin in the left hand.

The illustration on the right shows where to place the coin in the right hand.

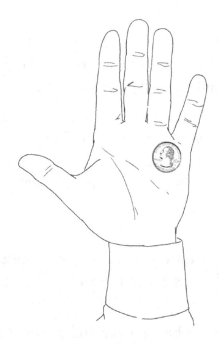 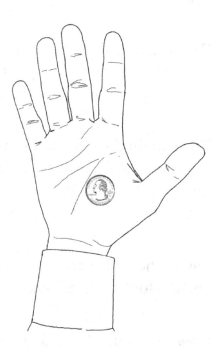

A Hole in One

This is an easy to do coin trick. It does not require any sleight of hand or difficult technique. This trick will add variety to your routine.

Effect: The magician borrows a quarter from a spectator. The spectator is asked to mark the coin so that he will be able to identify it later. The magician explains that he has a hole in his pants pocket and that money keeps falling out of it. He demonstrates this by dropping the marked coin into his right pants pocket. He then says that the interesting thing is that the hole is not in the right pocket but the left pants pocket. To prove it he lifts up his left foot to show the coin!

Setup: The setup for this trick is really simple. All you need to do is place a quarter under your left foot before you do the trick. This can be done while you are doing another trick. "Accidentally" drop some item on the floor, such as a piece of paper, a card from a card routine, etc. While you are retrieving the item, place the quarter under your left foot. If you do your magic while sitting at a table, this is very easy to do. If you are doing magic while standing up, you can use a large piece of paper (something you might use in another trick) to cover the action of placing the coin under your shoe.

Performance: Borrow a quarter from someone in the audience. (This routine can be done with any denomination of coin. Just ask the spectator for the same denomination of coin that you placed under your left foot). Have the spectator mark the coin with a felt-tip marker. This can be a letter X, his initials, a number, or whatever he chooses to use to identify the coin later during the routine.

Take the coin from the spectator. Say, *"Thank you for letting me borrow your quarter. I have been losing a lot of these lately. You see, I have a hole in my pants pocket, and my money keeps falling out. I'll show you."* Place the quarter in your right pants pocket. Pull out your hand to show it's empty. (This will remove any doubt that you might be palming the coin.)

Grab some pants material above your right pants pocket and shake it, as if you are shaking out the coin through a hole in the pocket. Follow the make-believe motion as if the coin was actually falling out of the hole in your pocket to the floor.

Say, *"However, the craziest thing is that the hole is not in my right pants pocket but my left pants pocket. So the coins always fall over here."* As you finish saying this, lift up your left foot to show the coin. Reach down, pick up the coin, and place it in your right pocket. Switch it for the spectator's marked coin. Say, *"You probably want your coin back. I was hoping I could keep it because as you have just seen, they keep falling out of my pocket!"* Give the spectator his coin. (The spectator will always look at it to see if his mark is on the coin, so you do not have to say anything about it.)

The Hypnotized Half

This is a quick but very visual effect. It can be done anywhere in your routine. This small illusion plays big!

Effect: The magician hands out a half-dollar to a member of the audience, who examines it. He then takes the half-dollar and stands it upright in the palm of his hand. When he lets go of it, the half-dollar remains in the upright position. The magician "hypnotizes" the coin to make it lie down in his hand.

Setup: To perform this trick, you will need a small piece of wire, about an inch long. A piece of a paper clip will work just fine, but a thinner diameter of wire is even better.

Performance: Have the small piece of wire concealed in your right hand. You can do this easily by curling your fingers around it. Hand out a half-dollar for examination. Do this with your right hand, and it will further eliminate the audience's suspicions about any type of gimmick that might be used in the trick.

Take back the coin with your right hand. With your left hand, place the wire behind the coin. Hold the coin upright. Your left fingers will be in front of the coin, and your left thumb will be pressing the wire up against the back of the coin (The coin will hide the wire from the view of the audience.)

Place the coin and the wire so that the wire is held between the first joints of your right index and middle finger. The wire will hold the coin in an upright position. Say, *"Watch closely."* Then let go of the coin with your left hand. (Hold the coin so that it is facing the audience. The coin will hide the wire.) It will appear to the audience that the half-dollar is defying gravity by standing upright.

Say, *"I will now put the coin to sleep."* Use your left hand to make a "hypnotizing" motion with your fingers. Say, *"Sleep,"* as you *SLOWLY* relieve the pressure of holding the wire with your fingers. The coin will slowly lie down on your palm.

Pull your right hand back toward you. Slightly open your fingers so that the wire will fall into your lap. Hand out the coin for examination.

The Hypnotized Half

The illustration on the left shows how the coin would look to the spectator.

The illustration on the right shows the coin from the back. This is the magician's view, and the coin conceals the pin from the view of the spectator. Note that the pin is holding the coin upright. To make the coin fall, simply relax the grip on the pin. The pin will fall between your fingers.

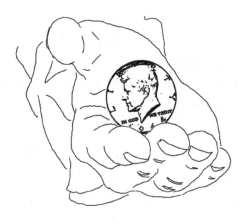 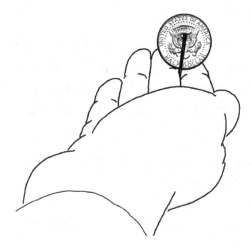

The Magic Circle of Coins

This is a self-working coin trick that is very easy to do. The use of a lot of coins makes it a very visual effect. Coins are borrowed from the audience, which makes it even more magical!

Effect: The magician borrows several coins from members of the audience. He places them in a circle. He then makes a tail with a few of the coins. The layout would look like a letter Q, with the tail on both the inside and outside of the circle. The magician turns his back. He asks a spectator to think of a number and to count around the circle of coins to that number. The spectator then counts around the circle to whatever his number was. The spectator notes which coin he stopped at. The magician turns to face the audience and amazingly, he reveals which coin the spectator stopped at!

Setup: No setup is required for this trick. It can be done with borrowed coins of any denomination.

Performance: Say, *"I would like to borrow some coins from the audience. I need about twenty of them, but I'll take whatever we can put together."* It is important that you have between fifteen and twenty coins. Make sure you have coins with you in case the audience does not have any. It is always better to use coins supplied by the audience so they will not be suspicious of gimmicked coins. It does not matter which denomination of coins are used. An assortment of different coins only adds to the presentation.

Take five coins and place them in a straight vertical line on the table. Now place the other coins in a circle so that the five coins are like a tail in a letter Q, with the tail going inside and outside the circle.

Now select one spectator and say, *"Think of a number between ten and twenty. This is a completely free choice, and I will not influence you in any way. Do not tell me what the number is. While my back is turned, silently count out on the coins to the number you are thinking of. Start counting with the coin at the bottom of the tail."* Point to the coin that is on the bottom of the row of coins. *"Count around clockwise until you get to your number. Stop there, and then starting with that coin, count back counterclockwise around the circle ... but count over the coins in the tail."* Show him how to count over the tail by skipping over the line of coins and resuming the count on the other side of the line of coins. *"When you get to your number, remember which coin you stopped at."*

Turn your back while the spectator does this, and say, *"Let me know when you're done."*

When the spectator is finished, turn around to face the audience. You will automatically know which coin the spectator stopped at because it will ALWAYS be the fifth coin to the right of the tail. Instead of just telling him at which coin he stopped, it is important to make the revelation as dramatic as possible.

Say, *"There is no way possible that I could know the number you chose, so there is no way possible that I could know which coin you stopped at. However, maybe I can use the energy you used when you were counting the coins to help me."*

Hold your hand up over the coins. Close your eyes, as if you are concentrating very deeply. Slowly move your hand around the circle, as if you are feeling for the energy of the coin. Go around the circle in a clockwise motion, and then stop and go around counterclockwise. Stop in the area where the selected coin is. (Of course, this will be the fifth coin to the right of the coins that are in a straight line.) Bring your hand down over the selected coin and say, *"Yes, this is your coin!"*

The Magic Circle of Coins

The illustration below shows how to lay out the coins on the table. Note that there are five coins in a straight line or tail. It is important to use somewhere between fifteen and twenty coins.

The spectator should start counting clockwise at the bottom of the tail (these are the five coins that are in a straight line), as shown by the dotted line. Once he stops at his selected coin, he now counts counterclockwise. It is important that he skips over the five coins that are in the straight line.

No matter which number he originally chose, the spectator will always stop on the fifth coin to the right of the straight line of coins.

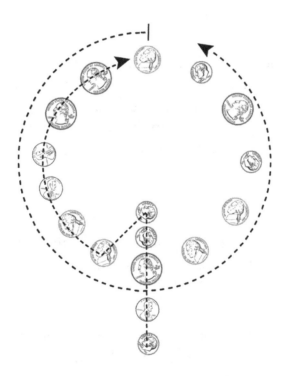

Into Thin Air!

This is one of the easiest coin vanishes ever. Practice it, and you will have a trick that you can perform anytime and anywhere.

Effect: The magician shows a coin in his right hand. He places it in his left hand and closes his hand. He snaps his fingers over his left hand to show that the coin is gone. He also opens his right hand to show that the coin is really gone, as if it disappeared into thin air!

Setup: There is no setup required for this trick.

Performance: Show a coin of any denomination to your audience. Let them take it and examine it thoroughly. Take the coin back with your right hand. Open up your left hand with the palm up.

Make a motion to place the coin into your left hand but at this time, drop the coin. Here's where the magic happens. With a natural movement, bend down to pick up the coin. With a natural movement, slowly stand up while bringing your hand toward your shoe, and drop the coin in between your sock and shoe. Do this movement very smoothly and in one continuous movement. I have performed this routine hundreds of times, and the audience has never noticed this movement.

Continue the movement of standing up. Immediately cup your left hand and act as though you are dropping the coin into your left hand. Close the fingers of your left hand to make a fist around the "coin."

Use your right hand to snap your fingers over your closed left hand. Hold your clenched left hand up to your ear, as though you can still hear the coin as you shake your left fist. Snap your right fingers over the left fist again.

Snap the fingers of your left hand and open your left hand to show the coin is gone. Snap the fingers of your right hand, and show the right hand is empty. This will have a startling effect on your audience as it seems the coin has vanished into thin air!

Top Five

Everyone loves magic with money! This is an easy to perform effect that I am sure will become one of your favorite impromptu tricks. As a blind magician, I like tricks like this because they are simple to perform and do not need any setup.

Effect: The magician borrows a one-dollar bill and a five-dollar bill from members of the audience. He places the one-dollar bill on top of the five-dollar bill. He then rolls the bills together into a small tube. He asks a spectator to put his finger on the one-dollar bill to make sure it stays on top of the five-dollar bill. However, with a snap of his fingers, the magician unrolls the bills, and now the five-dollar bill is on top of the one-dollar bill!

Setup: No setup is required for this trick.

Performance: Ask the members of the audience for the use of a one-dollar bill and a five-dollar bill. (This trick can be done with any denomination of bills as long as you use two different denominations. For example, a ten- and twenty-dollar bill.)

Place the one-dollar bill vertically and center on top of the five-dollar bill (which is horizontal). The bills now make an upside-down letter T formation.

Say, *"Please note that the dollar bill is on TOP of the five-dollar bill."*

Starting at the bottom edge of the bills, roll them together in an upward roll. Continue doing this until the five-dollar bill is rolled up all the way and in a tube shape.

Stop rolling, and ask a spectator to put his finger on the one-dollar bill. Say, *"Nothing has happened yet. Your finger will help keep the one on top of the five."*

Then say to the spectator, *"Did you feel the magic happen?"* Of course, he will say no. Say, *"Well, something magical happened because the five is now on top of the one!"* Simply unroll the bills to show that the five-dollar bill is now on top of the one-dollar bill.

Top Five

The illustration on the left shows how to lay the one-dollar bill on top of the five-dollar bill.

The illustration on the right shows how to roll the five-dollar bill forward and over the one-dollar bill.

The illustration on the left shows how to keep rolling the five-dollar bill (and the one-dollar bill that will be rolled inside) into a tube. Continue doing this until the other edge of the five-dollar bill is on the top of the tube.

The illustration on the right shows that when the bills are unrolled, the five-dollar bill is now on top of the one-dollar bill.

Silver Express

This is a very visual trick (although you do not have to have vision to perform it). It is self working and easy to do. Once you practice folding the paper you will have a trick that you will love to perform!

Effect: The magician borrows a quarter from a spectator. He asks the spectator to mark the coin. The magician then seals the coin in a piece of paper. The sealed coin in the paper is placed in full view of the audience. With a snap of the fingers, the magic takes place. The magician announces that the coin has vanished from the sealed paper. To prove this, he tears the paper into little pieces. He then produces the spectator's marked coin from his pocket!

Setup: A borrowed coin can be used for this trick. You will also need a felt-tip marker and a small piece of paper that measures about five inches by five inches.

Performance: Borrow a quarter from someone in the audience. (A half-dollar or an Eisenhower dollar works great with this trick. It is my experience, however, that in most instances, no one will have either of these coins.) Ask the spectator to mark the coin so he will be able to identify it later. Show the small piece of paper, and let the spectator examine it.

Hold the quarter in the center of the paper with your left thumb and fingers. Say, *"I am now going to seal the coin in the paper. Please watch."*

While holding the coin (clipped between your left thumb and fingers) in the center of the paper, fold the top of the paper back toward you so that the top edge of the paper is now about a half-inch below the coin. DO NOT FOLD THE TOP EDGE EVEN WITH THE BOTTOM OF THE PAPER. Crease the paper at the top of the now-enclosed coin. This will seal the coin at the top. Say, *"As you can see, the coin is sealed on the top."*

Now hold the paper over the sealed coin with your right thumb and fingers. With your left hand, fold the left side of the paper away from you, so that the crease is about a quarter-inch away from the left side of the coin. Crease the paper and say, *"It is now sealed on the left side."*

Now hold the paper against the sealed coin with your left thumb and fingers. Fold the right side of the paper away from you so that the right edge of the fold is about a quarter-inch from the sealed coin. (The paper will overlap the left-side fold.) Crease the right-side fold and say, *"It is now sealed on the right."*

Hold the paper against the sealed coin with your right thumb and fingers. Here is where the magic comes in: Fold the bottom of the paper *AWAY* from you. (Do not fold it toward you, or it will actually seal the coin in, and the trick will not work.) You will now have a slot in the paper where the coin can slide out, but it will appear to the audience as if the coin is sealed inside the paper. Make sure to hold the coin tightly so that it does not fall out of the slot. Say, *"The coin is now sealed from the bottom. The coin is completely sealed in the paper."*

Take the coin in the sealed paper and rap it on the table so the audience can hear it. Now, as you lift the coin up from the table, let the coin slide into your right hand. Your fingers will cover this move. Curl the fingers of the right hand around the coin. (This is called a Finger Palm.) Keep the coin hidden in your hand as you grab the paper with your left hand. As your left hand places the paper on the table, drop your right hand down below the table. (Do this naturally and in a relaxed manner.) Put the coin in your pocket.

Say, *"Please watch closely."* Snap your fingers over the paper. Say, *"Magically, the coin has vanished."* Pick up the paper, and tear it into small pieces. Let the pieces fall to the table. Say, *"I am sure you would want your coin back. And here it is."* Reach into your pocket and give the spectator his coin. You will not need to ask the spectator to look at the coin to see if his mark is on it. It is my experience that he will do this automatically.

The illustration below shows where to place the coin. It is placed in the center of the paper.

Silver Express

The illustration on the left shows how to fold the piece of paper over the coin (fold the top edge back toward you). Fold the top edge over so that it covers the coin. Do not bring the top edge of the paper to the bottom edge. Leave a space below the coin.

The illustration on the right shows how the paper is folded on both sides of the coin. Do not fold the paper up against the coin. Leave a little space so the coin will slide out easier. Fold both sides to the front (away from you).

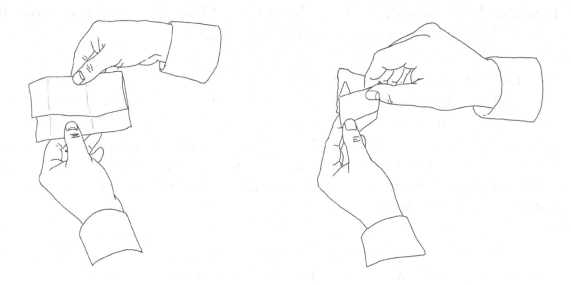

The illustration on the left shows how to fold the bottom edge of the paper. Fold it forward. This will appear to the audience that you have sealed the coin on all four sides. However, this last fold leaves an opening that enables the coin to slide out of the paper.

The illustration on the right shows how to pull the paper up while letting the coin slide into your hand. Your fingers will conceal the coin from the view of the audience.

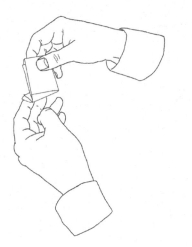
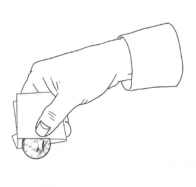

Compound Interest

This is an easy to perform coin trick. It requires no difficult or complicated moves. It is great for impromptu magic.

Effect: The magician tells the audience how compound interest works. He says that it is a way that money makes money. To demonstrate this, he shows a penny in one hand. He passes his hand over the penny, and the penny changes into two dimes!

Setup: You will need two dimes and a penny.

Performance: Before you show the trick, you need to place the coins in an exact position in your right hand. Place the two dimes between the index finger and thumb of your right hand. The dimes should be in line with the fingers. Now place the penny in front of the dimes. From the front, the penny should cover the dimes so they cannot be seen by the audience.

Hold the coins at the eye level of the spectator or audience. You must make sure the audience only sees the penny and not the two dimes. (If the coins are held above or below eye level, the two dimes can be seen). Say to the audience, *"I am sure you have heard about compound interest. It basically is a way that money makes money. I would like to demonstrate this for you using this penny. If I were to invest this penny for a long time, it could grow, and I could double my money. Please watch."*

Show that your left hand is empty. Reach over with the left hand. Push on the bottom of the penny with your left thumb. At the same time, rotate the two dimes so that you now have a stack of coins. At the same time, slide one dime off the stack with your left thumb and left index finger. The right thumb and forefinger will now have the dime in front of the penny.

Move your left hand to the left, displaying the dime. The audience will see a dime in one hand and a dime in the other. (They will not see the penny that is now concealed by the dime.) Say, *"I seem to have done better than just doubling my money!"*

Let the two coins in between your right thumb and right index finger fall back into the palm of your hand. The fingers of that hand will cover the coins from the view of the audience. Drop the coin in your left hand into your right hand, on top of the other two coins. Put the coins in your pocket.

Compound Interest

The illustration below shows how the penny would look to the audience. The penny is held so that it conceals the two dimes that are behind it.

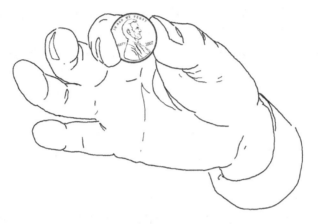

This is a view looking down at how the two dimes are held behind the penny.

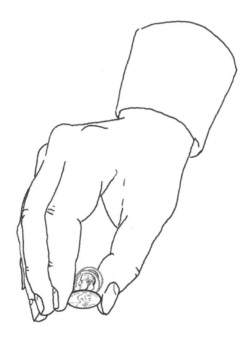

It's in the Mail!

This is a fun trick to perform. It is easy to do, and there are no difficult sleight of hand moves.

Effect: The magician shows an envelope. He then removes a dime, a nickel, and a penny from the envelope. He gives the envelope to a spectator to place in his pocket. The magician shows the three coins, and one is made to disappear. Magically, it reappears in the envelope that the spectator has kept in his pocket!

Setup: You will need two dimes, a nickel, and a penny for this trick. You will also need a handkerchief (a cloth table napkin will work, too) and a small envelope. I use 3⅝ by 6½-inch security envelopes, but a coin envelope will work well also. Put the extra dime in the envelope, and let it slide to one corner. Now put the other three coins (the dime, the nickel, and penny) in the corner on the other side of the envelope. Fold the envelope in half to keep the coins apart. I also put a stamp on the envelope and put my return address on it. This makes it look more ordinary.

Presentation: Show the audience the envelope, and take out the dime, the nickel, and penny. Set the coins down on the table. Fold the envelope and ask a spectator to put his finger on it. (This will keep him from feeling the envelope and exposing the dime inside.) Say, *"I would like you to guard the mail."*

Pick up the three coins on the table. Put them between your left thumb and left fingers. Hold them at the bottom of the coins, but let the dime stay a little bit above the nickel and penny. Say, *"As you can see, I have sixteen cents—a dime, a nickel, and a penny. If I wanted to send one of these coins through the mail, it would cost me forty-four cents (this is the cost of a postage stamp in 2010). It doesn't seem like such a good deal to me, so I developed a method of magic 'air mail.' Please watch closely."*

Cover the coins with the handkerchief. Use your right thumb and right fingers to grasp the handkerchief on top of the coins. Say, *"The magic will now take place."* Quickly lift up the handkerchief. Of course, the coins are still there. Say, *"Oh, I forgot to say 'airmail.' I'll do it again."*

Cover the coins again. Grasp the coins through the handkerchief as before, only this time, grasp only the dime. Say, *"Airmail"*, and quickly pull off the handkerchief (along with the dime). Immediately focus your eyes on your left hand. The audience will assume that nothing has happened, just as before. At this time, drop the handkerchief and the hidden dime to your right side, and place the dime inside your pocket. By focusing your attention on your left hand, you will provide misdirection so the ditching of the coin will not be noticed by the audience.

Say, *"Believe it or not, the magic HAS taken place."* Drop the nickel and penny on the table. Say, *"You see, all I needed to send away was the dime. As you can see, it is now gone."*

Ask the spectator who has his finger on the envelope to lift up his finger and open the envelope. Amazingly, the dime is in the envelope!

The illustration below shows how the coins should be placed in the envelope. A dime is placed on one corner, and a dime, nickel, and penny are placed in the other corner of the envelope.

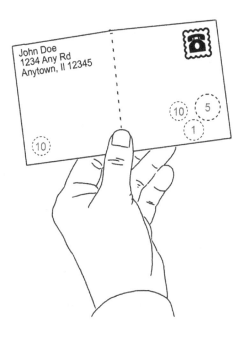

It's in the Mail!

The illustration on the left shows how the nickel, dime, and penny are held by the hand that is underneath the handkerchief. Note that the dime is a little higher than the other two coins.

The illustration on the right shows how the handkerchief is draped over the hand. The coins are held as before, with the dime a little higher than the other two coins.

Counterfeit Connection

I love this trick! It is one of my favorites, and I am sure it will become one of yours. It is easy to perform and a real audience pleaser.

Effect: The magician displays several bills and asks a spectator to select one of them. The selected bill turns out to be the only bill that has the word COUNTERFEIT written on the back!

Setup: You will need six one-dollar bills for this trick. On the back of three of the bills, write the word COUNTERFEIT. You can write this in pencil if you want to use the bills later on. Alternately, you can write COUNTERFEIT on a piece of masking tape, stick it on the bills, and simply remove the tape later. Now stack the bills with a regular dollar bill on top, then a "counterfeit" bill, a regular bill, a counterfeit bill, a regular bill, and a counterfeit bill on the bottom. Arrange all the bills with George Washington's face showing and the top of his head to the left. You are now all set to perform the trick.

Performance: Bring out the stack of bills. Fan them out to show they are all one-dollar bills. (You can fan the bills out as wide as you want, as you don't have to worry about flashing the counterfeit bills.)

Say to a spectator, *"Are you good with money?"* Whatever the answer, say, *"Let's see. Please freely choose any one of the bills."* For instructional purposes, let's say the spectator chooses the fourth bill down in the stack. (Only you know this is one of the counterfeit bills.)

Take off the three bills on top of the selected bill and place them on the bottom of the stack. (Make sure to retain the order of the bills you put on the bottom.) You now have a stack of bills in your left hand (one of the "counterfeit" bills is on top of the stack).

Set the top bill on the table. Say, *"You really are good with money because you selected the only counterfeit bill in the stack."* Turn over the bill on the table so the spectator can see the word counterfeit on it.

Now here is the real magic: You now will show the rest of the bills as "good" bills. Here's how you do it. Hold the bills in your left hand. Take off the top bill with your right hand (this will be a good bill). Hold the bill in your right hand with your thumb on top and your fingers on the bottom. Hold the stack in your left hand with your left thumb on top and your left fingers on the bottom.

Now turn your palms toward you so that your palms face downward. By doing this, you will show the back of the bill in your right hand and the back of the bottom bill in the stack, which is in your left hand. Turn your palms back to the original palm-up position.

Set the bill in your right hand down on the table. Immediately place the top bill in your left hand on top of the bill on the table. (You have now set one of the counterfeit bills on top of a good bill, but the audience assumes you showed the backs of both bills.) Now repeat this. Take the top bill from the stack, and put it in your right hand. Turn both hands over to show the bottom of the bills. Set the bill in your right hand on top of the bills on the table, and then place the top bill on the stack on top of the stack that is now on the table. This will leave you with a "good" bill in your left hand. Show the back of it, and place it on top of the stack that is on the table.

Note: If the spectator selects a good bill, then do the same thing, only this time show that he selected the only "good" bill. Use the method above to show the rest of the bills as *ALL* counterfeit bills.

The illustration below shows you how to stack the bills. This would be the view if the stack of bills were turned over at the start of the trick.

A Visit to the Mint

This trick will add a nice variety to your coin routine. It is easy to do, and there are no difficult moves to learn.

Effect: The magician explains that the U.S. Mint is responsible for printing up money. He uses a dollar bill for an example and folds up the bill. He also explains that the U.S. Mint makes coins. With that, he tips the dollar bill—and a half-dollar falls out!

Setup: You will need a dollar bill and a half-dollar to perform this trick. Put the bill and the half-dollar into your right pants pocket or jacket pocket.

Performance: With your right hand, reach into your pocket and pull out the dollar and half-dollar. Hold the coin behind the bill, using your right thumb to hold the coin up against the bill. Bring out the dollar with the coin concealed behind it.

Show the dollar bill to the audience. Say, *"As most of you know, the U.S. Mint is responsible for printing money like this dollar bill."* Snap the left side of the bill with the fingers of your left hand.

Now grab the left side of the bill with your left hand. Push the coin from the right side of the bill over to your left thumb. Your left thumb (and left fingers that are on the front side of the bill) now grip the coin. Snap the right side of the bill with the fingers of the right hand. The audience will now assume that both hands are empty and that there is nothing gimmicked with the bill.

Fold the coin in the bill by folding the bill over from right to left, and then fold it top to bottom.

Say, *"While most people know the Mint makes paper money, some people do not know that it also makes all the coins ... like this one."* Slowly tilt the folded bill and let the half-dollar fall out on the table. Your audience will be astonished at this production!

A Visit to the Mint

The illustration on the left shows you how to hold the half-dollar behind the dollar bill. This would be the magician's view at the back of the dollar bill.

The illustration on the right shows how to push the ends of the dollar bill together to push the middle of the dollar bill outward. As you do this, transfer the half-dollar to the left side of the dollar bill. Simply grasp it with your left thumb and hold the coin to the left side.

The illustration on the left shows the half-dollar on the left side of the dollar bill. This is the view the magician would see.

On the right is an audience view of how the bill appears. The bill conceals the half-dollar.

Magical Money Maker

This is a very visual effect that plays big. It really is an attention getter and becomes a favorite of any audience.

Effect: A magician hands a handkerchief to the audience to examine thoroughly. (Better yet, he could borrow a handkerchief from someone in the audience.) The magician takes the handkerchief and produces an endless number of coins!

Setup: You will need two identical coins (I use two Kennedy half-dollars) and a handkerchief to perform this trick. It is always better to borrow a handkerchief from someone in the audience. However, it is my experience that many times no one in the audience has a handkerchief. So, let the audience thoroughly examine your handkerchief. Put one of the coins in your right pants pocket and the other coin in your left pants pocket.

Performance: Ask to borrow a handkerchief from someone in the audience. If they do not have one, show them yours, and let them examine it thoroughly.

Take the handkerchief back and gracefully pull the handkerchief over both of your open hands. This is a good way to show that your hands are empty. Put the fingers and thumb of your right hand together and point them up. With your left hand, drape the handkerchief over the right hand.

Reach over with your left hand and grab the top of the handkerchief. Now flip the handkerchief over your left hand so that the handkerchief is over the upward fingers and thumb of the left hand. (All you have done is switched the handkerchief from the right hand to the left.)

Look at the top of the handkerchief. Say, "*What's that?*" Look puzzled, as if there is an invisible coin on top of the handkerchief. Reach over with your right hand, and put your hand around the "invisible coin." Put the invisible coin in your right pocket and as you do so, take the real coin and slide it into the curled-up middle finger, ring finger, and little finger. (This is known as a Finger Palm.) Bring out your hand naturally and casually. Keep your fingers curled around the coin, and it will be concealed from the view of the audience.

Look at the top of the handkerchief that is now draped over your left hand. Grab the top of the handkerchief with your right hand, and flip the handkerchief over your right hand. (Remember to keep the back of the right hand toward the audience so you do not flash (expose) the coin that you are holding in the right-hand Finger Palm position.)

Once again, look at the top of the handkerchief (which is now in the right hand), as if there is an invisible coin on top of it. Grab the invisible coin with your left hand, and put it in your left pocket. This time, put the coin in your left pocket in the Finger Palm position. Bring out your hand in a natural motion.

With the index finger and thumb of your left hand (the other fingers are concealing the coin in the Finger Palm position), grab the top of the handkerchief in your right hand. At the same time, also take the coin by pinching it through the handkerchief. Flip the handkerchief back over the upward fingers (which are also pinching the coin) of the left hand. You will now have one coin outside the handkerchief and one concealed beneath the handkerchief in the Finger Palm position of the left hand.

Slowly push the coin up with your left thumb and index finger, which is on the outside of the handkerchief. Push it up slowly, as if the coin is magically materializing from nowhere.

Reach over with your right hand and take the coin. Place it into your right pocket, but retain the coin by putting it in the Finger Palm position. Bring your hand out of the pocket with the concealed coin.

Now just keep repeating this process. Reach over with your right hand and grab the top of the handkerchief (and the coin that was concealed in the left hand). Flip the handkerchief over the right hand. Once again, slowly push up the coin on the outside of the handkerchief. Take the coin with your left hand and place it in the left pocket. Once again, retain the coin in the Finger Palm position. Bring out the left hand with the concealed coin.

Repeat all the same moves as above. Grasp the handkerchief with the left hand and flip it over the left hand, and once again take the coin that was concealed in the right hand.

Do these back-and-forth moves, and it will appear to the audience as if you are producing an endless supply of coins. When you are finished, give the borrowed handkerchief back to the spectator and say, *"Thanks—that's a real moneymaker!"*

Magical Money Maker

The illustration on the left shows how the coin is concealed under the little, ring, and middle fingers. This is a Finger Palm position and is used in many coin tricks.

The illustration on the right shows the hand underneath the handkerchief. One coin is held at the fingertips on the outside of the handkerchief. The other coin (shown by the dotted line) is concealed in the hand in the Finger Palm position.

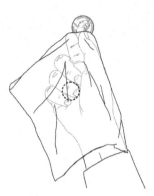

In the Money!

This is a very visual trick that you will love to perform. It is a great impromptu money trick, and it plays big with an audience. It is, in fact, a mini-illusion!

Effect: The magician shows a dollar bill and a blank piece of paper. He folds the dollar bill and then folds the piece of paper so that it encloses the bill. The magician then sticks a pencil through the bill and the paper. He slides the pencil down and through the hole that he punched in the bill and paper. He snaps his fingers and opens the folded bill. Although there is a hole in the paper, there is no hole in the dollar bill!

Setup: You will need to prepare a dollar bill to perform this trick. Take a sharp object a make a vertical slit (top to bottom) on the right side of the small circle that is to the right of the image of George Washington. This is the seal that sometimes has a letter, such as a G or D, in it. The slit should be made in the dark circle that surrounds the letter. If cut properly, the tiny slit will not be seen by the audience.

You will also need a blank piece of paper. A piece of blank typing paper or note paper will do just fine. Cut the paper to about the same size as the dollar bill (it does not have to be exact). You will also need a sharpened pencil.

Performance: Bring out the bill, paper, and pencil. Fold the dollar bill in half from side to side. (As you are looking at George Washington, fold the right side over to the left side.) Now fold the top half from left to right. By doing this you will cover the little slot in the bill. (The slot will be covered about a quarter-inch by this front flap.)

Take the paper and fold it around the bill so that the bill is inside the paper. The bottom fold of the paper should be folded at the bottom fold of the bill. Lift up the flap of the dollar bill, and crease the paper fold. Now fold the flap of the bill back over the paper. You can now see the dollar bill, but the small slot is covered by the flap.

Say to the audience, *"Please watch closely."* Take the pencil and slowly push it through the slot. Keep going and punch through the paper. The audience will assume the pencil is going through the *DOLLAR* and the paper. Push the pencil up and down a few times for added effect. Grab the bottom of the pencil, and pull it all the way through.

Snap your fingers and say, *"Some people don't like money with holes in it."* Unfold the dollar and the paper. Show the dollar to have no holes in it. (The audience's attention will be focused on the center of the bill, as that's where they think the hole should be. This will provide even more misdirection, focusing attention away from the slot in the bill.) Show the hole in the paper.

In the Money!

In the illustration below, the dotted line shows where to cut the small slot in the dollar bill. Make sure it is big enough to push the pencil through.

The illustration on the left shows you how to fold the paper and the dollar bill. Note that the slot that is in the dollar bill is below the fold.

The illustration on the right shows how the pencil is pushed through the slot that is in the dollar bill. It will appear to the audience that the pencil penetrates the dollar bill and the paper. However, the slot allows the pencil to slide behind the dollar bill.

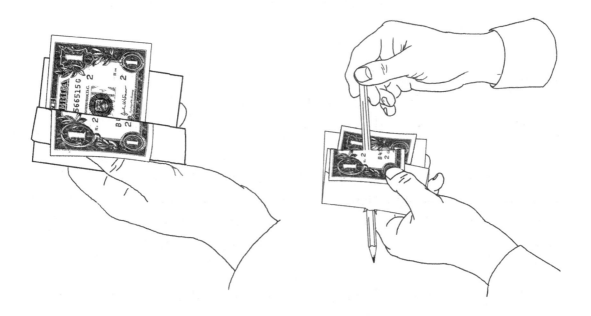

Smooth Move

This is a smooth and graceful way to vanish a coin. Practice it before you perform it before an audience. This instant coin vanish is impressive.

Effect: The magician drapes a handkerchief over a coin that is held in his fingertips. He pulls the handkerchief over the coin and when the handkerchief is pulled completely over the coin, the coin will have vanished!

Setup: You will need a coin (I use a quarter but any denomination will do) and a handkerchief. You will also need to be wearing a shirt or jacket that has a breast pocket on the left side.

Performance: Show the audience a quarter by pinching it between your right thumb and index finger. The face of the coin should face the audience.

Hold one of the corners of the handkerchief with your left index and middle fingers.

Drape the handkerchief over the coin. Slowly but with a continuous motion, pull the handkerchief back toward you. When you come to the coin with your left hand, pinch the coin between your left thumb and index finger. DO NOT HESITATE. Make this one graceful, continuous movement. Keep your right thumb and fingers in place, just as if the coin was still there.

Continue slowly pulling back the handkerchief with the coin clipped between your left thumb and index finger. Now, drop the coin in your breast pocket. DO NOT HESITATE. Drop the coin in the pocket while still slowly pulling on the handkerchief.

Keep pulling the handkerchief until it is over the fingers of your right hand. When the handkerchief clears the right hand, look directly at the right thumb and fingertips (this is where the coin was). Act as surprised as the audience to see that the coin has now vanished! Gently shake the handkerchief, and let it drop on the table.

Note: The key to this trick is the continuous movement. Practice this until you can do it gracefully and without hesitation.

Smooth Move

The illustration below shows the handkerchief in the magician's left hand. The coin is held by the fingertips of the right hand.

The illustration on the left shows the handkerchief being brought back to the jacket or shirt pocket so the coin can be dropped in the pocket.

The illustration on the right shows the coin (shown by dotted line) in the pocket.

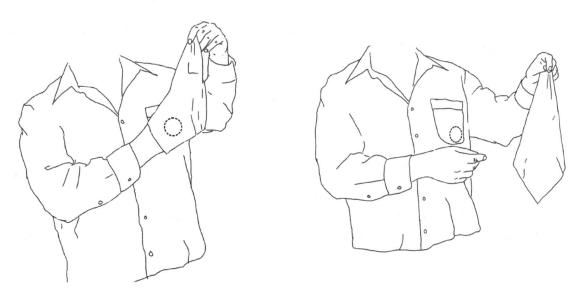

Gone—but Not for Long!

This trick is a real reputation maker! The time and effort it takes to practice is well worth it in performance impact. This is one of my favorite tricks and works especially well in an impromptu situation.

Effect: The magician borrows a half-dollar from someone in the audience. The spectator marks the coin for later identification. The magician makes the coin vanish and magically reappear again!

Setup: You will need a felt-tip marker. (If you don't have a marker, a pencil or pen will work just as well. I prefer using a felt-tip marker, as it leaves a permanent mark on the coin, and I also use the marker in other tricks.) You will need to wear a suit coat or jacket. Place the marker in the inside pocket of the jacket.

Performance: Ask to borrow a half-dollar from someone in the audience. If no one has a half-dollar, a quarter will work fine. While you can do the trick with any coin, I would suggest not using a dime, nickel or penny—they are too small to be seen by the audience.

Say to a spectator, *"Please mark the coin so you can identify it later."* Pull the marker out of your coat and give to the spectator.

Note: Bring your left hand up to the left side of your jacket and pull out your coat to get the marker. Reach in and get the marker with your right hand. This is important, as you will be repeating this same motion later in the trick. By doing it always the same way, it conditions the audience and provides a natural movement when you later use this motion to "sleeve" the coin.

Take the marker back and place it inside the jacket pocket. Take the coin and put it in the palm of your right hand. Toss the coin over to the left hand, and then toss it back to the right. (Practice tossing the coin from hand to hand so you can do it in a smooth, confident way.) Toss the coin from hand to hand three or four times. Just make sure it winds up in the left hand. Keep your left hand closed but palm up.

Reach inside your jacket (just as you did when you gave the spectator the marker to sign the coin) and get the marker. Say, *"I'll use my marker as a magic wand."* Tap the back of your hand with the marker. Say to the spectator, *"Choose heads or tails."* (It does not matter what the spectator says, as this is done for presentation only.)

Open your left hand to show the coin. If the spectator guessed the side correctly, say, *"You could be a magician!"* If the spectator didn't get it right, say, *"Oh, I see. You made your choice when I was tapping on the back of my hand. In that case, the coin was turned over, so you are right! That's amazing!"* In either case, say, *"Good. Let's see if you can do it again."* Put the marker back in your jacket, just as you did before. Put the coin in the palm of your right hand.

Once again, toss the coin from hand to hand. Now, here's where the magic comes in: As you toss the coin from your right hand, close your right middle, ring, and little fingers around the coin (this is the Finger Palm position). It is important to keep the same tossing motion, as if you are really throwing the coin over to the left hand. Act as if you are catching the coin in your left hand, and close it in a fist as you did before. Practice this move so you can do it casually and naturally. It should be one smooth motion, and it will appear to your audience that you have just tossed the coin into your left hand, as you did previously.

Now just like before, reach inside your jacket to get the marker. Remember to use your left hand. (The audience will assume the coin is in your left hand, so just use your index finger to help pull open your jacket. Keep the other fingers closed, as though you have the coin closed up in your palm.)

Here's the other secret move: As you reach with your right hand to get the marker from inside the jacket, simply drop the coin down the sleeve of the jacket. Your left hand (which is holding open the coat) will be in the perfect position to do this, as the back of your left hand will be facing the audience and will provide cover from the view of the audience. Let the coin slide down the sleeve (between the jacket and your shirt) until it falls to your elbow. Do not worry about the coin falling out, as you will keep your arm and elbow slightly bent upward during the rest of the trick.

Take out the marker with your right hand. Once again, tap on the back of your left hand. Turn your left hand over and ask the spectator, *"Once again, is it heads or tails?"*

No matter what the spectator says, pause for a moment. Slowly open the fingers of your left hand. (I do this by opening one finger at a time.) Act as shocked as the spectator to see that the coin has disappeared.

Hand the marker to the spectator. Now just snap the fingers of both hands, hold them open, and turn them over, so the audience can see that both hands are empty.

Very slowly and naturally, lower your left arm. The coin will slide down your sleeve. Cup your left hand, and let the coin fall into your hand. Close your left middle, ring, and little finger around the coin (the Finger Palm position). While doing this, reach for the marker with your right hand. This will provide misdirection so the audience won't notice what is happening with your left hand.

Say, *"Please watch closely."* Tap the back of your left hand with the marker in your right hand, just as you did before. Turn over your left hand slowly and, as before, open your hand, one finger at a time, to reveal the coin. Ask the spectator to examine the coin for his mark. This is a very startling effect for your audience!

The illustration on the left shows the coin in the right hand, as seen by the audience. The right hand moves toward the left hand as you toss the coin over.

The illustration on the right shows another audience view. The coin has been tossed back over to the right hand. The dotted line shows how the coin is retained in the right hand in the Finger Palm position.

 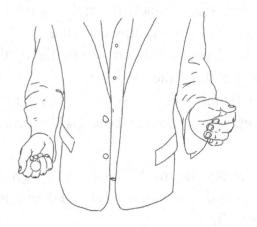

Gone—but Not for Long!

The illustration on the left shows how the coin is dropped into the left sleeve. The dotted line shows how the coin drops toward the elbow.

The illustration on the right shows how the coin is dropped when the left arm is straightened out. The dotted line shows how the coin travels down the arm into the palm of the left hand.

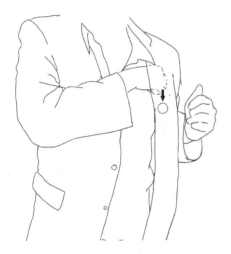
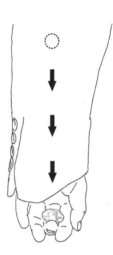

Right on the Money!

This is a nice impromptu trick that requires no complicated technique. It is self-working, and it will add variety to any close-up magic routine.

Effect: The magician lays three coins of different denominations on the table. He then tells the spectator that he has a prediction in his closed right hand. The spectator is asked to choose a coin. The magician opens his hand to show that his "prediction" is the same denomination coin as the spectator's chosen coin.

Setup: You will need a dime, a nickel, and two quarters. Before you perform the trick, put the quarter in your right hand and close your fingers around it. Do this out of the view of the audience.

Performance: One of the quarters is already closed up in your right hand (the audience does not know this). Select a spectator from the audience. Place the three coins down on the table. Say to the spectator, *"How many coins are down on the table?"* He will answer three. Now say, *"And what denomination are they?"* He will say a nickel, dime, and quarter.

Say, *"Good. I have a prediction in my hand."* Show him your closed-up right hand. *"I would now like you to choose one of the coins on the table, and slide it toward me."*

Now here's the magic: If the spectator slides the quarter toward you, slowly open up your right hand and show your prediction. Say, *"Wow, you must be a magician, too!"*

If the spectator slides the dime toward you, say, *"Okay, there are two coins left* (the quarter and the nickel). *This is the important choice. Choose one of the coins, and slide it toward you."* If the spectator slides the quarter toward himself, say, *"Good, that's your choice."* Then reveal the quarter in your hand as described earlier. If the spectator slides the nickel toward himself, say, *"Good, that leaves the quarter."* Open your hand to show your prediction.

If, after the coins are first placed on the table, the spectator selects the dime or nickel, proceed the same way. For example, let's say he first selects the nickel and slides it toward you. Say, *"Good. Now, this is the important selection. I want you to choose one of these coins."* Point to the quarter and the dime. If he chooses the quarter, then show your prediction. If he chooses the dime, say, *"Good, that leaves the quarter,"* and then show your prediction.

This is called *"Magician's Choice,"* because no matter which coin the spectator selects, you will use the quarter as his "choice." Slowly open your right hand to make the revelation of your prediction more dramatic!

Bread Money

This is a great trick if you do table magic or restaurant magic. It also makes a great impromptu trick for dinner with friends. The audience will really love it!

Effect: The magician picks up a dinner roll from the table. He breaks open the roll and produces a half-dollar!

Setup: You will need to be at a table on which there is a dinner roll, breakfast roll (such as a cinnamon roll or Danish roll), cupcakes, or other bread items. You will also need a half-dollar (the trick will work with any coin but a half-dollar is more visible to the audience and makes for a better performance).

Performance: Place a coin in the palm of your right hand. Place it so you can conceal the entire coin with your middle finger and ring finger. If you also curl in your little finger you will have the coin in the Finger Palm position. Practice concealing the coin in this manner so you can move your right hand naturally and relaxed.

Pick up the roll with your left hand, with your thumb on top of the roll and the fingers on the bottom of the roll. Bring the roll to your right hand. Place the roll on top of the coin (which is concealed in your right hand). Let the coin slide down toward the fingertips of the right hand as you break open the roll.

Slowly break the roll in half by tearing it from the top to the bottom. Do this by pushing up with the fingers of both hands from underneath the roll, while tearing the roll apart at the top. Use the middle finger and ring finger of the right hand to push the coin into the bread at the bottom (push the coin up through the bread). Leave the bottom part of the roll together when pushing the coin up through the bread. This makes for a more magical production of the coin. It will look like the coin has materialized from inside the bread! When the coin is at the top, say, *"Wow, I found some bread money!"*

Grab the coin and pull the roll completely apart in two pieces. This will remove the hole that was created by pushing the coin up from the bottom.

Bread Money

The illustration on the left shows how to put the coin in the Finger Palm position. Curl your middle, ring, and little finger over the coin to conceal it. You can extend your index finger and thumb freely. Practice this until you can move your hand (with the concealed coin) in a natural manner.

The illustration on the right shows the right hand holding the dinner roll. Note that the coin is still concealed in the Finger Palm position.

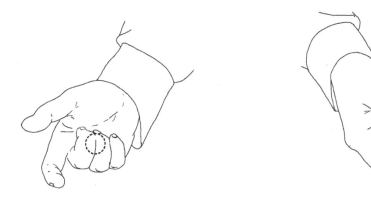

The illustration on the left shows how to tear the bread apart while pushing the coin upward through the bread.

The illustration on the right shows the coin as it appears in the bread.

Coin Through the Table

This is a classic of magic. The world famous magician Tony Slydini invented the trick and taught it to me. I met Slydini at a magicians convention (Magic Desert Seminar). A special lecture offered the privilege of learning from one of the greats of magic. Slydini lectured on three of his most famous effects: Coin through the Table (Slydini was well-known for his expertise in lapping technique), the Dissolving Knots (a beautiful effect, in which two silks are tightly tied together and placed in a glass, only to have the knots magically become untied when the silks are taken out of the glass), and Flight of Paper Balls (a great effect in which paper balls are made to disappear, right before a spectator's eyes, in a very funny presentation). While I can do this effect, I will never be able to do it like Slydini. He was so very charming and such a nice person. He was very kind to me and told me that as a blind magician, I could be an inspiration to others. Slydini was truly an artist in every sense of the word. He performed magic in the way that an artist paints on a canvas. He would tell a story with the magic—and therein was the greatest lesson I ever learned about magic: Magic is not about the way the trick works. It is about how the trick is performed.

This trick will be a nice addition to your close-up magic routine. Practice it many times before you perform it, and you will have an effect that you will really love to perform. It is great for table magic and impromptu magic situations.

Effect: The magician shows a half-dollar. He slaps the coin on the table. He then finds a "hole" in the table. The coin is then produced from under the table. The other hand that once covered the coin is lifted to show that the coin did, in fact, go through the hole in the table!

Setup: You will need two identical coins. I use half-dollars, as they are more visible to the audience. However, the trick could be done using two quarters. You must also sit down to perform this version of the trick. Before you begin, secretly place one of the half-dollars in your lap. Make sure it is hidden from the view of your audience.

Performance: Show the audience the identical half-dollar. Place it in the palm of your left hand. Say, *"Believe it or not, some of these tables have a hole in them. I'll show you."*

Slap your left hand (and the coin) down on the table. Do this about ten inches from the edge of the table nearest you. Show that your right hand is empty. Reach under the table with your right hand. As you do this, grab the coin that is in your lap. (Practice this move many times so you do not hesitate when grabbing the coin. It should be one continuous, smooth motion).

With your right hand, go to the spot under the table that is directly under your left hand (which is on top of the table).

Now here's where the magic happens: Move your left hand toward the center of the table. While doing this, slightly lift up the back of your hand so that the coin can stay where it is. Just move your left hand forward toward the center of the table, and let the coin end up under your arm (your arm will cover this move).

Note: While moving your hand forward, slide the coin, which is in your right hand under the table, along the path of your left hand. This will make the sliding sound of the coin, and the audience will assume the coin under your left hand is making the sound.

Now immediately bring out your right hand, showing the half-dollar, and drop it on the table. As soon as you do this, slide your left arm back toward you, and allow the coin that is under your left arm to fall in your lap.

Pick up the coin on the table with your right hand and toss it into your left hand. This shows that your left hand is empty, and it is also a good way to direct attention away from the motion you just made by "lapping" the coin under your left arm.

Practice this routine many times before you perform it. It should be done very smoothly, relaxed, and graceful.

Coin Through the Table

The illustration below shows how to begin with the coin on the table. The coin is near the back edge of the table.

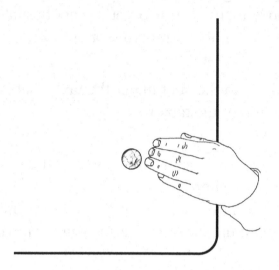

The illustration on the left shows how to make it appear that you are pushing the coin toward the center of the table. However, the coin actually stays under the forearm. The audience will assume the coin is still under your hand.

The illustration on the right shows how the coin is pulled back when you pull back your arm. Let the coin fall off the table and into your lap.

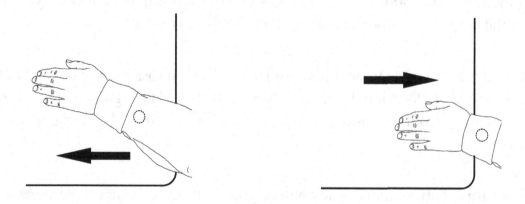

Magical Multi-Money Prediction

This is a very visual coin prediction trick. Since people like tricks involving money, they will love this trick!

Effect: The magician pours out a dollar bill and several different coins from a small coin envelope. He then has a spectator freely select one of the coins. Amazingly, the magician correctly predicts the chosen coin!

Setup: While this is a self-working trick, there is some preparation needed. You will need a:

1. small coin envelope
2. dollar bill
3. half-dollar
4. quarter
5. dime
6. nickel
7. penny

The secret of the trick is to be able to predict any coin the spectator chooses. Here's how it's done: On the coin envelope, write the following on the side opposite the envelope flap: YOU WILL SELECT THE PENNY.

Fold the dollar bill in half by bringing the right edge over the left edge. Now fold it in fourths by once again folding the right edge over to the left edge. Write "YOU WILL SELECT THE DIME" on a white adhesive label, and place it on the bottom fourth of the folded dollar. Now open the top fourth of the dollar. On the left fourth, place a label on it that reads: YOU WILL SELECT THE NICKEL. Now unfold the bill and place a label on it that reads: YOU WILL SELECT THE HALF DOLLAR.

Cut a piece of an adhesive label and place it on one side of the quarter. Write "YOU WILL SELECT THE QUARTER" on the label. Now place all these items in the coin envelope. Make sure the dollar is folded and placed so that none of the predictions are exposed when it is poured out of the envelope. Make sure the prediction side of the quarter is down and is not exposed when it is poured out of the envelope. Also make sure the envelope always has the blank side facing the audience so the prediction side is not exposed. Once you have prepared the trick, you are ready to perform it. This is a nice trick to carry with you, and you will always have a routine in your pocket.

Performance: Pour the contents of the coin envelope out on a table. Make sure none of the predictions are showing. Place the dollar bill down so that it looks like a normal folded-up bill. Make sure you place the coin envelope with the prediction side down. Say to the audience, *"I would like to show you a trick that I do with several different coins. This is what I have—a half-dollar, a quarter, a dime, a nickel, and a penny. I am so sure that I will get this trick right I am willing to bet money on it."* Tap on the dollar bill.

Say to a spectator, *"I would like you to choose any coin. It is a free choice, and I will not influence you in any way."* Let him select a coin. Say, *"Are you satisfied with your selection, or would you like to choose another one?"* (As you know, it really doesn't matter what the spectator chooses. However, giving him the chance to change his selection adds to the impact of the prediction.)

If the spectator chooses the dime, simply turn over the folded-up dollar to let him see the words "YOU WILL SELECT THE DIME."

If the spectator selects the nickel, simply open up the top flap to show the label that reads "YOU WILL SELECT THE NICKEL."

If the spectator selects the half-dollar, unfold the dollar completely to show the label that reads "YOU WILL SELECT THE HALF-DOLLAR."

If the spectator selects the quarter, have the spectator turn over all the coins except the quarter. Then say, *"Would you now turn over the quarter?"* When he does, he will see the label that reads "YOU WILL SELECT THE QUARTER."

If the spectator selects the penny, say, *"I took all these coins out of this envelope. Please turn over the envelope and read what is on it."* He will turn it over and read, "YOU WILL SELECT THE PENNY."

After the routine, pick up all the coins and the bill without exposing any of the other predictions. Be careful to place the envelope in your pocket without exposing the prediction that is written on one side.

Magical Multi-Money Prediction

The illustration below shows how to mark the adhesive tape that you put on the quarter. It should read "YOU WILL SELECT THE QUARTER." It also shows you what to write on the back of the envelope. It should read "YOU WILL SELECT THE PENNY."

The illustration below shows how to fold and mark the dollar bill. Fold the bill into fourths and mark one of the flaps so it reads "YOU WILL SELECT THE DIME." The other flap (as shown) is marked "YOU WILL SELECT THE NICKEL." The back side of the bill is marked "YOU WILL SELECT THE HALF-DOLLAR."

Mental Magic

Magic of the Mind

Mental magic is referred to as mentalism. Just as with card or coin magic, there are magicians who do only mental magic. They are referred to as mentalists. While mentalism may use some standard magic methods and effects, it is the performance that separates a magician from a mentalist. Correctly done, the audience is more focused on the performance and outcome of the performance than on the method or technique of how the mentalist accomplished the effect.

Mental magic has been around for many years. Some mentalists were so convincing with their performances that the audience thought they had special powers. This is a real tribute to the talent of the mentalist that he gains the confidence of the audience.

Many magicians have one or two mental magic effects in their routines. It is very well suited for stage magic. If you would like to learn advanced mentalism effects, I recommend that you check your local library for books on mentalism or magic books that have a mental magic section. There are also many videos and DVDs that specifically deal with mentalism.

The Nose Knows!

Let's begin mental magic with an easy effect. This trick does not depend on any type of props or gimmicks. It depends more upon human nature or involuntary reaction than it does magic technique. Try it a few times, and you will see for yourself. As mentalism depends a lot on presentation, this trick will impress the audience with your ability of ESP (extra-sensory perception).

Effect: The magician borrows a coin from someone in the audience. A spectator is asked to put his hands behind his back and place the coin in one hand. The spectator is told to keep the coin hidden in his fist and then to bring his arms up by holding them straight out to the side. Amazingly, the magician is able to tell the spectator which hand the coin is in!

Setup: There is no setup for this trick. It may be done with a borrowed coin. This is a great trick in an impromptu situation.

Performance: Ask to borrow a coin (any denomination will do) from someone in the audience. Select a spectator and say, *"I would like you to put your hands behind your back, and put the coin in one hand. I will turn my back while you do this, so there will be no way I can possibly determine which hand you use. Let me know when you have the coin in one hand."* Turn your back to the spectator. Take your time, as this is part of the buildup of the presentation.

When the spectator tells you that he has the coin in one of his hands, turn and face him. Say, *"Good. Now put your arms straight out to the sides."* As soon as he does this, do not look at his hands—look at his nose! It will actually point to the hand that contains the coin! I don't know why this works, but it does. Try it on your friends, and see for yourself.

Note: Casually look at his nose. Do not let him be aware that you are looking at his nose.

As soon as you see which hand his nose is pointing to, close your eyes, as if you are concentrating. For instructional purposes, let's say his nose pointed to the right. This means the coin is in the right hand. Very slowly, say, *"The coin is in your right hand.*" When he asks you how you knew which hand the coin was in, say, "*Highly developed extra-sensory perception.*"

If for some reason you get it wrong, don't worry about it. Act as though it is perfectly normal and turn it into a comedy prediction. Simply say, "*Of course, you must remember that you put the coin in your left hand when my back was turned. So when I turned around, my left hand was on your right side. So technically, I was correct!*" The audience will laugh at this, and this is a good way to get your audience relaxed. Either way, this trick will please the audience.

It's in the Numbers!

This is a great prediction trick that will work great in any mental magic routine. It is very easy to do and makes a great audience participation trick.

Effect: The magician takes a small piece of paper and seals it inside an envelope. He then asks members of the audience to call out single-digit numbers. The magician writes down the numbers on the envelope. He eventually stops them and then asks someone from the audience to add up the numbers. The spectator is then asked to open the envelope and read what is on the piece of paper. It correctly matches the total!

Setup: You will need a small piece of paper and an envelope for this trick. Write any number on the slip of paper. I use the number thirty-four. I would suggest using a number over twenty-five and no more than forty. Put the piece of paper in the envelope and seal it up. You are now ready to perform the trick.

Performance: Ask the audience to call out some one-digit numbers. The same number can be repeated. Write the numbers down in a column on the envelope. As the numbers are called out, add them up mentally.

Remember, the prediction number is thirty-four (or you may have a different number), so let the audience keep giving you numbers until they add up to twenty-seven (or the number can be higher). Say, *"Good—that's plenty. I'll make a line to make it easier for someone to add these up."* Since you stopped the counting at twenty-seven, you simply add a seven to the column as you make the line under the numbers. (This will of course bring the total to your prediction number to thirty-four.)

Now hand the envelope to a spectator and ask him to add up the numbers. When he adds the numbers, the total will be thirty-four. Say, *"Please open up the envelope and read my prediction."* The spectator and audience will be amazed that the prediction is the same as the total of the audience numbers!

Mind-Power Prediction

This is a great trick to add to your mental magic routine. It is an audience favorite.

Effect: A spectator is asked to select a card. He then returns the card somewhere in the deck. Amazingly, the magician knows which card was selected!

Setup: Because there is some setup needed for this trick, I think it should be used as an opener for your routine. You can then use the cards later for another effect.

The setup is simple: Take all the even cards (2, 4, 6, 8, and 10) and the Queens and put them in a separate pile. Shuffle them to mix them up. Now take the other cards (the odd cards—1, 3, 5, 7, 9—and the Jacks and Kings), and put them in another pile. Shuffle them to mix them up. Turn the cards face down, and put the first pile of cards (the even cards and Queens) on top of the other pile (the odd cards, Jacks, and Kings). You are now ready to perform the trick.

Performance: With the deck of cards in your left hand, spread the *top half* only. Ask a spectator to choose a card. If he insists on selecting a card from the bottom portion, then reverse these instructions. Most people, however, will choose a card from the top portion. Say, *"Please look at the card and remember it. Do not tell me what it is. Are you satisfied with that card, or would you like to make another selection?"* This adds to the presentation and helps the spectator and the audience realize this is not a forced card.

Say, *"Good. Then replace it somewhere back in the deck. I will turn my head so I won't know where you put it."* Turn your head away. Just spread out the *bottom half* of the deck. Let the spectator put his chosen card in this bottom half. Square up the deck.

Turn the cards face up, and spread out just the *bottom half* of the deck. You will be able to determine the spectator's chosen card immediately, as it is the only even-numbered card (or a Queen) among the odd cards, Jacks, and Kings. Take the card from the deck, and place it face down on the table.

Say, "*As you know, you had a completely free choice of selecting a card. There is no way possible that I could know which card you selected. You put it back in the deck in a random location, and I did not influence you in any way. It is truly a matter of reading your mind. Now, what was your card?*" The spectator should announce the card he selected. Then say, "*Please pick up the card on the table, and tell everyone what it is.*" The spectator and audience will be astonished to see that the card is the spectator's chosen card!

Mind-Power Prediction

Note: As mentioned, if a spectator insists on selecting a card from the bottom half of the deck, just make sure to return it to the top half of the deck. Then all you have to do is look through the top half to find the card.

The illustration below shows how to set up the cards. The even cards and Queens are to the left, and the odd cards and Jacks, Kings, and Aces are on the right. Note that the cards on each side are mixed up so they do not appear to be stacked.

The illustration below shows you how to fan out the cards so the spectator can choose a card. The top portion (the even cards and Queens) are spread out so the spectator will choose from this portion. As the spectator is looking at the card, spread the bottom portion (the odd cards, Jacks, Kings and Aces). Have the spectator put his card in this bottom portion of cards.

Mind-Power Prediction

The illustration below shows how easy it is to know which card the spectator selected. In this illustration, the Two of Diamonds is the only even-numbered card among the odd cards. Note that because the cards in each portion are in a random order, the deck looks like it has not been set up or stacked.

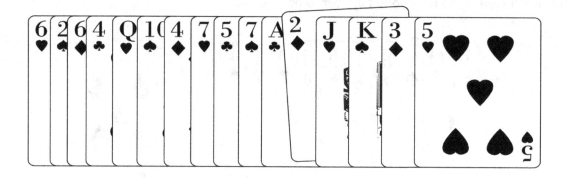

That's Impossible! Book Test

It seems that many mental magic routines have a book test effect. There are many different types of book tests and different methods. This is one of the easiest. This effect will leave quite an impact on your audience.

Effect: The magician asks a spectator to choose a word from a dictionary. The choice is random and is in no way influenced by the magician. Somehow, someway, the magician is able to correctly reveal the spectator's chosen word.

Setup: The setup for this trick is quite simple. You will need two exact copies of a small dictionary. They should be small enough to fit into your pocket. These can be purchased at just about any bookstore. The two I have are small Webster's dictionaries. They are small enough to fit in my shoe! Just conceal one of the dictionaries on you. You can put it in your pocket, inside your jacket, or wrap it around your leg with a rubber band.

Performance: Have one dictionary concealed on you before performing the trick. Pick out a spectator from the audience. I do this by turning around so my back is to the audience. I toss a small paper ball over my shoulder for someone to catch. I then tell whoever caught the paper ball to hand it to anyone in the audience. Then I tell that person to hand the paper ball to someone else. All this helps to add to the effectiveness of the trick. This eliminates any ideas the audience might have about their being a confederate (hidden assistant) in the audience.

Ask the chosen spectator to name any number between one and whatever the number of pages are in the dictionary. Let's say there are 150 pages. Then ask the spectator to think of a number between one and whatever number of lines of print there are on a page. Let's say there are thirty-five lines of print in the dictionary. Let's assume the spectator says page 101, line twenty-two.

Say, *"I would now like you to turn to page 101 and count down to line twenty-two, and find the word that begins that sentence. I will go in the other room while you do this so there can be no way I might determine which word you find."* Go into another room. You might say, *"This is a good time for me to use the restroom. Once you find your word, write it down on the piece of paper and fold it up."*

Because you know the page and line number the spectator chose, it is a simple matter to look up the word in your hidden dictionary. Return to the room, but before you enter, say, *"Have you finished writing the word down? Have you folded up the paper? Good."*

Enter the room. Sit down and say, *"May I touch the piece of paper, please?"* Touch the paper, and then close your eyes, as though you are concentrating very deeply. Slowly say the chosen word. Your audience will be stunned by the revelation!

That's Your Word

A magazine test is very similar to a book test. There are many different methods used to perform this trick. I think this is one of the easiest magazine tests to learn. It will work great in your mental magic routine.

Effect: The magician shows the audience a sealed envelope. He hands the envelope to someone in the audience. He then shows the audience a magazine. He asks a second spectator to put the magazine behind his back and to then mark a page with an X that goes from corner to corner. The magazine is handed back to the magician. The magician then asks the first spectator to open the sealed envelope and to read what is written on the card that is inside. The magazine is handed to the second spectator, who is asked to find the page he marked with the X. He is then asked to read the word aloud that is directly under where the two lines of the X intersect. Amazingly, it is the same word as the one written on the card in the sealed envelope!

Setup: It is important to select a magazine that has some pages with mostly words on them. It also should be a magazine with which the audience is familiar. The reason for this is simple. If it is a magazine they do not recognize, they might be suspicious of a gimmicked magazine.

The page with mostly words should be close to the middle of the magazine, and it should be on the right side. Take a felt-tip marker, and draw an X on the page from corner to corner.

As the spectator will be drawing the X behind his back, do not make the X too perfect. Practice drawing an X on a piece of blank printer paper to give you an idea of what the X should look like. It would not be straight and might be curved. Make the X so that it intersects one word. Make sure it does not intersect in the exact center of the word, or it will look too gimmicked.

Take a blank card (like an index card), and write the word that is in the intersection of the two lines. Take the card and seal it in an envelope.

You will also need a felt-tip marker that does not work. This can be done very easily by leaving the cap off the marker for a few days. (In fact, you could use the same marker that you use for the "X Marks the Spot" card trick that was explained in the Card Magic section.) I would also recommend applying some clear fingernail polish on the tip of the dried-out marker. This will ensure that it will not leave any ink marks. You are now ready to perform the trick.

Performance: Show the audience the sealed envelope. Hand it to someone in the audience. Ask another spectator to help you. Show the second spectator the magazine and say, *"I would like you to select a page at random in the magazine. To make it completely random, do this with the magazine behind your back."*

Let the spectator put the magazine behind his back and then find a page. Say, *"Keep the magazine behind your back, and mark an X across the page from corner to corner."* Show the spectator how you want him to do it. Tell him to fold over one side of the magazine and put an X on the other page. (Saying this will ensure that the spectator makes the X on the right side).

Note: I actually use the magazine to show the spectator how to fold it open and how to make the X. If you do this, it is important you do not show the page with the X already on it.

Hand the marker to the spectator. Say, *"When you're done, close up the magazine and hand it to me."* When he hands the magazine and marker back to you, put the marker away. Say, *"Ladies and gentlemen, when I began, I gave a sealed envelope to someone in the audience. Please remember this was given to him before I had the second spectator make a mark in the magazine."* Say to the spectator holding the envelope, *"Please open the envelope and read out loud what is written on the card."*

Now give the magazine back to the second spectator. Say, *"Please thumb through the magazine until you find the page you marked."* Give the spectator time to find the page. Then say, *"Good. Please read out loud the word that is located where the lines of your X intersect."*

The spectators and the rest of the audience will be as amazed to see that the second spectator's word matches the word that was sealed in the envelope!

That's Your Word

The illustration below shows how to mark the X on the magazine page. In the illustration, the word NEWS has the X through it. This would be your prediction word.

Amazing Mind Transposition

Here is another variation on the book test. This is a unique book test that is very easy to do. It will add variety to your mental magic routine. This is one of my favorites. I sometimes use it when I perform stage magic.

Effect: A spectator is given a choice of two books. After the spectator chooses a book, he is asked to cut a deck of cards. He takes the top two cards from the deck and adds the numbers together to determine a page in the book. The magician asks the spectator to go to that page and briefly read it to see what it is about. The magician then announces to the audience that he will "channel" the mind of what the character in the book is thinking! The magician then proceeds to describe, in detail, what the character is saying or thinking about.

Setup: You will need two books. I would suggest using novels that have a storyline. Do not use textbooks, cookbooks, picture books, etc. Pick a page in one of the books that is within eighteen pages from the front of the book. This page should include the name of a character in the book, as well as narrative about what the character is doing or thinking. This will be your force page.

You will also need a deck of cards. Take out the number cards that add up to the number of your force page. For example, if your force page is 10, then take out a number 6 and a number 4 card. For instructional purposes, let's say the force page is 17. Take a number 9 card out of the deck and a number 8. Place these two cards on top of the deck. You are now ready to perform this fantastic trick!

Performance: Select a spectator from the audience. Ask the spectator to choose one of the books. If he chooses the force book, give it to the spectator to hold. If he chooses the other book, say *"Okay, this is the one I'll use."* (This is a very simple form of Magician's Choice. It helps the audience to think it is a completely random choice). Either way, you will use the force book.

Take the cards out of the card box. (Only you know the two force cards are on top of the deck. If you wish, you can give the deck a false shuffle and retain the two force cards on top. (Use the false shuffle you learned in the Card Magic section.)

Say to the spectator, *"Please cut the cards anywhere you would like, and set the two halves on the table."* Let the spectator cut the cards.

Take the bottom portion of cards, and set them down at an angle on the top half (the half that has the two force cards on top). This is to set up the deck for a simple force. Say, *"Good. You had a completely free choice of where to cut the cards."* Lift the upper portion of cards (the portion that is at an angle on top of the other cards), and set it down on the table. Push the bottom portion of cards forward (only you will know that this portion has the two force cards on top), toward the spectator.

Say, *"Now, take two cards off the top and remember what they are. I will turn away so there is no way I can know which cards you select."* After this is done, say, *"Now I would like you to add up the numbers of the cards you chose, but don't tell me what the total is."* Give the spectator time to do this.

Turn around and say, *"Whatever the total was, I would like you to turn to that page number in the book."* (Only you will know this is the force page.) Say, *"I would now like you to briefly read over that page so you can get a good idea of what the page is about."* Give the spectator a few minutes to do this.

Then say, *"And now, ladies and gentlemen, I would like to do something I think you will find rather amazing. I am going to channel the thoughts of the character in the book and read the mind of the character!"*

Act as though you are concentrating very deeply. Then go into detail about what the character in the book is saying, doing, or thinking. Do this very slowly and dramatically. For example, you might say, *"The character in the book is a ... a lady. She recently moved to ... New York City. She is thinking about ... she is thinking about how fortunate she is to have found a nice job in a bank. Her name is ... Helen."* Look at the spectator and ask, *"Is that correct?"* Of course it will be, and the spectator and the audience will be completely stunned!

Note: To further add to the effect, I actually give away the book. I tell the spectator that he might like reading the rest of it. This really takes the suspicion away that the book might be gimmicked in some way. You do not have to do this, but this is how I perform the effect.

Amazing Mind Transposition

The illustration below shows how to set the bottom portion of cards on the top portion of cards. Only you will know that the top two cards on the bottom portion are the force cards.

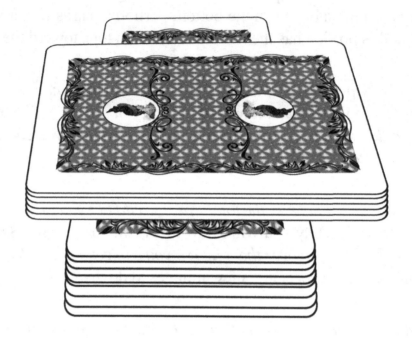

Mind Over Matter

This is a great trick to do for a table magic routine. It is easy to learn, and you will enjoy performing it. It will add variety to your mentalism routine.

Effect: The magician picks up several different objects from the table. He places these down in front of a spectator. He asks the spectator to concentrate on one of the objects. The magician then picks up a butter knife. He taps on the object while the spectator silently spells out the letters of the object he selected. Somehow, the magician ends up on the object the spectator selected.

Setup: While there is no special setup used in this trick, you must have certain objects and remember them in the following order:

1. cup
2. fork
3. plate
4. pencil
5. quarter
6. envelope

The magic of this trick is in the list. Note that each object has one more letter than the previous object. (Cup has three letters, fork has four letters, etc.) You may substitute different objects as long as they have the same number of letters. For example a plate (five letters) could be replaced by a spoon (five letters), or a fork (four letters) could be replaced with a dime (four letters). This will enable you to use a wide variety of objects, depending on what is available.

Performance: Pick up several objects from the table and put them in front of a spectator. Say, *"As you can see, I have ..."*—count as though you are counting to yourself—*"one, two, three, four, five, six, seven, eight objects. I would like you to concentrate on one object, but don't tell me what it is. Once you have done this, write it down on this piece of paper, and put the paper in your pocket. I will turn my back so I will have no idea which object you choose."*

Turn back around and say, *"I would now like to use this butter knife as a magic wand. Actually, I just need it to tap on these objects. When I tap on an object, I would like you to spell out, silently in your head, each letter of your object with every tap I make. When you come to the last letter of the object, say Stop. For example, if you selected the fork, it would be f-o-r-k, and you would say Stop on the letter K. Do you understand?"*

Begin to tap slowly on any two objects. Then make sure the third object you tap on is the cup. The fourth item would be the fork, the fifth the plate, and so on down your list. When the spectator says stop, you will be tapping on the object he selected. Say in a very dramatic way, *"That IS the object you chose. Could you show everyone what was written on the paper?"* Of course, it will prove you correctly stopped on the spectator's selected object.

Magical Mystery Revelation

This is a great audience participation trick, and it really baffles an audience—it seems impossible.

Effect: The entire audience is used in this effect. The magician shows the audience a small object. Then he turns his back to the audience. One of the audience members hides the object in his pocket. The magician turns around and scans the audience to pick up a special "energy." He then reveals who has the hidden object.

Setup: This is one of the few tricks in this book that uses a confederate, or secret assistant. Many mentalism effects use a confederate, but it must not be overdone. By using a confederate, it will appear to the audience as if you have special mystical powers. This is because the trick seems so impossible.

You will also need a small object. Stay away from ordinary objects, like coins, keys, pens, etc. You could use an item such as unusual jewelry, a charm from a bracelet, a small medallion, etc. I feel it is important to use something that is not commonplace, as it makes for a better presentation. I use a small piece of crystal. Some people believe crystal has special energy or power, and this just helps to add to the presentation.

You can use one of your friends or family as your secret assistant. Just tell him to never reveal the secret. Most people love to be *"in"* on the trick, as it makes them feel special to be part of a trick that seems so impossible. Have your secret assistant in the audience.

Performance: Show a small object to the audience. For instructional purposes, let's say the small object is a crystal. Hand it to someone in the audience and say, *"I am going to turn my back."* In some instances, you might want to go into another room, but this is not necessary. *"I would like you to pass around the object, and I would like someone to hide it in his or her pocket."* Your secret assistant will watch closely to see which spectator puts the object in his pocket.

Wait a few minutes to allow the object to be passed around and hidden. Turn around and say, *"It is impossible for me to know who has the hidden object."* While you are talking, your secret assistant is copying the actions of the person who has the hidden item. For example, if the person puts her hand on the back of a chair, so does your secret assistant. If the person crosses his hands in front of him, so does your secret assistant. You may also work out other indicators with your secret assistant. Such as, if the person sits down in a chair, your assistant would sit down to the right of or stand at the right side of the person. There are many different ways the assistant can indicate who has the hidden object.

Once you know who has the hidden object, say, *"I will see if I can pick up on the special energy of the object."* Close your eyes and act as if you are concentrating. Hold your hand with the fingers up and palm toward the audience. Move it back and forth, as if you are scanning the audience.

Eventually, stop scanning, and when your hand is pointing directly at the person with the object, say dramatically, *"You are the person who has the crystal!"*

Triple Telepathy

This is a great mentalism effect. It is easy to do and fun to perform. It plays big, and your audience will love it!

Effect: A spectator shuffles a deck of cards, cuts the cards into two stacks, and then selects one of the stacks. The spectator then gives three cards to three other spectators. The magician "reads the minds" of each spectator and then tells each one what his card is!

Setup: No setup is required for this trick. It can be done with a borrowed, shuffled deck.

Performance: Ask a spectator to shuffle a deck of cards. Take the cards and spread them out, saying, *"Let's make sure there are no Jokers in the deck."* While doing this, look at the second, third, and fourth cards from the top of the deck, and memorize them. Do this naturally and without bringing attention to it. Square up the deck, and set it on the table.

Say to the spectator, *"Please cut the cards into two piles. You can cut them anywhere you like. It is a completely free choice."*

After the spectator cuts the cards into two stacks, say, *"Which stack of cards do you want me to have?"* If the spectator selects the stack of cards that has the three known cards under the top card, say, *"Good. That's the one we'll use."* If the spectator selects the other stack of cards, say, *"Good. And here's yours."* Push the other stack (the half with the three known cards under the top card) toward the spectator. This is a simple form of Magician's Choice. Either way, the spectator or you will wind up with the top half of the deck.

Say to the spectator, *"Please take the top card off and place it somewhere in the middle of the deck. This will eliminate any doubt that I could somehow know which card it is and use it in some way."* (This will leave the three cards you memorized on the top of the deck.) *"Now, please choose three different spectators from the audience. This is your choice, and I do not want to influence you in any way. Please give each of the three spectators a card from the top of your stack of cards."* (Only you will know that the three spectators will receive the three cards you memorized.)

Direct your attention to the three spectators. Say, *"I would like you to look at your cards but do not tell me or anyone else what the card is. Please concentrate on the card."*

Put your fingertips to your temple as though you are reading the minds of the three spectators. Then, one by one, tell each what his card is. This will be totally amazing to the spectators and to the rest of the audience!

The Mystery Key

This trick will add some variety to your mental magic routine. Many years ago I bought a trick at a magic shop called Key-rect. It used a gimmicked padlock to achieve the same effect as this trick, but in this version, you can use an ordinary padlock purchased from a hardware store. This is a trick your audience will remember for some time!

Effect: The magician shows a padlock, seven keys, and seven small envelopes. He shows that only one key will open the lock. He sets this key aside and lets the audience members try the other six keys. As they find out, the other six keys will *NOT* open the lock. The magician then has a spectator seal each key in its own small envelope and drop the envelopes into a paper bag. The spectator then shakes up the bag to thoroughly mix up the envelopes. The spectator takes a key out of the bag and hands it to the magician. The magician concentrates on the key and sets it aside. Several keys are handed to the magician until he picks up on the "energy" of a certain key. The magician hands this key to the spectator and amazingly, it is the key that opens the lock!

Setup: You will need to purchase a padlock (the small type of padlock used on gym lockers, toolboxes, garden sheds, etc.). Make sure the padlock has two keys. Take the lock to a locksmith (most hardware stores have a key department) and have six non-working keys made. Just tell the person making the keys that you want six keys that will not work in the padlock. These keys should be made out of the same type of key stock as the two that came with the lock. It is important for all the keys to look alike, but only two keys will actually open the lock. You can get all eight keys made from the same "key blanks." This will ensure that all the keys look the same.

You also will need small coin envelopes to put the keys in—you can purchase these at any office supply store. And you will need a small paper bag—an ordinary paper lunch bag that you can buy at any grocery store.

Seal one of the keys that will open the lock in one of the envelopes. Put a small dot on both sides of the envelope in the upper left corner and the bottom right corner. Do this with a pencil, and make a mark so that you can identify the envelope. However, do not make the mark so big or dark that it would be easily noticed by the spectator or the audience. (As a blind magician, I put a small tactile dot, much like a Braille dot, on the envelope. I can feel this quite easily.) Put the envelope in the paper bag. You are now ready to perform this great trick.

Performance: Select a spectator from the audience. Give the spectator the lock and the key that opens it. Tell him to open the lock with the key. Say, *"You will find that only this key will open the lock. Notice that from this point, I will not touch the lock, the keys, or the envelopes."*

Have the spectator lock the padlock. Say, *"I would now like you to try these six keys in the lock. You will find they won't open it. Also, let some other members of the audience see if the keys will open the lock."* After this is done, say, *"Now, place the one key that will open the lock in an envelope and then place it in the paper bag. Now place each of the six keys in envelopes, and place all of them into the bag. Now shake up the bag thoroughly to mix up the keys. I would now like you to reach into the bag, get an envelope, and hand it to me."*

Take the envelope you are handed, and put it up to your forehead so you can focus your concentration on the key. As you do this, look for the small mark on the envelope (which tells you which envelope contains the key that will open the lock). If the envelope the spectator handed you is not the one with the key, simply set it down on the table, and say, *"No, please hand me another envelope."*

Do this until you are handed the envelope that contains the key that will open the lock. Say, *"Yes, this is the one. Please open the envelope, and see if it will open the lock."* Of course it will, and your audience will be amazed!

The Card Predictor Trick

Prediction tricks work very well in mentalism routines. This is a self-working card trick that requires no difficult moves. You will enjoy performing this trick as much as your audience enjoys watching it!

Effect: The magician cuts the cards and correctly predicts the card that he cut to. Amazingly, he does this several times!

Setup: There is no setup for this trick. It may be done with a borrowed deck.

Performance: Shuffle the cards with the Overhand Shuffle. Hold the deck so you can see the faces of the cards. As you finish the shuffle, use your left thumb to push up the top card so you can glimpse it. Remember it. For instructional purposes, let's say the top card is the Queen of Hearts.

Set the deck on the table. Cut the cards about in half so that you have two stacks of cards. We will call the portion of cards that has the Queen of Hearts on top the top portion, and we will call the other stack of cards the lower portion.

Pick up the top card from the lower portion of cards. Hold the card so only you can see it. No matter what the card is—let's assume it is the Two of Spades say, *"I am going to use this card to name the top card over here."* Point to top card on the top portion. Set the Two of Spades back on top of the lower portion of cards.

Say to the audience, as you tap the top card of the top portion, *"This card is the Queen of Hearts."* Lift up the Queen of Hearts to show to the audience. Place the Queen of Hearts back on top of the top portion of cards.

Now take the lower portion of cards (the stack with the Two of Spades on top), and place it on top of the top portion.

Now, repeat the process.

Cut the cards into two stacks. Say, *"I will now use this card"*—point to the bottom stack—*"to name the card over here."* Point to the top stack of cards. Once again, pick up the top card on the lower portion of cards. Let's assume it is the Six of Clubs.

Say, *"This card is the Two of Spades."* Pick up the Two of Spades to show to the audience.

Your audience will be amazed at how you can predict which card is being cut to. Although this trick can go on forever, I would suggest you only do it four times. Too much repetition can cause the loss of excitement in the routine.

The Mind-Reading Mentalist

This is another great mental magic routine. It is very easy to do. You will enjoy performing this effect.

Effect: A spectator shuffles a deck of cards. The spectator selects a card, remembers it, and replaces it on top of the deck. The spectator then cuts the cards into two stacks of cards. The magician writes a prediction on a piece of paper. He seals this prediction in an envelope and puts it on top of one of the stacks of cards. He then places the other stack of cards on top of the envelope. The envelope marks the completed cut. The magician then picks up the portion of cards on top of the envelope and turns it so the bottom card is now face up. The spectator is asked to open the envelope and read the magician's prediction. Amazingly, the magician has correctly predicted the spectator's card.

Setup: There is no setup required for this trick. It can be done with a borrowed, shuffled deck. As a blind magician, I have to start the trick by knowing what the bottom card is. You will not have to do this, as you will be able to glimpse the bottom card. You will need a pen, a piece of paper, and an envelope for your prediction.

Performance: Ask a spectator to shuffle a deck of cards. Say, *"Feel free to shuffle them again so you are satisfied that the cards are thoroughly mixed up."*

Take the cards from the spectator. As you do, tilt the cards so you can casually glimpse at the bottom card. Do this naturally and without calling attention to it. For instructional purposes, let's say the bottom card is the Ace of Spades.

Say to the spectator, *"I would now like you to cut the cards anywhere you want. This is a free choice. I will not influence you in any way. Just set the cards you cut off down on the table."* When the spectator sets the cards down on the table, set the other cards you are holding down beside the cards the spectator set down. Make sure you remember which stack of cards was on top before the cut.

Say, *"I would now like to make a prediction."* Act as though you are in deep concentration and then write on the piece of paper "THE CARDS WILL BE CUT,

AND THE CARD AT THE CUT WILL BE THE ACE OF SPADES" (or whatever the bottom card was). Fold the piece of paper and seal it in the envelope.

Place the envelope on the top portion of cards. Then take the bottom portion of cards and place on top of the envelope.

Say to the spectator, "*You shuffled up the cards until they were thoroughly mixed up. You also cut the cards at a random place in the deck. There is no way possible that I could know how the cards were arranged after you shuffled them. And of course, there is no possible way that I could have known where you were going to cut the cards. Let's take a look at which card you cut to.*" Turn over the top portion of cards (the portion on top of the envelope). Say, "*You cut to the Ace of Spades.*"

Then say to the spectator, "*Please open up the envelope, and read out loud my prediction.*" The spectator will read the prediction—to the amazement of the spectator and the audience!

The illustration below shows how the envelope is placed between the two halves of the deck. There is also a side view of how the envelope separates the top and bottom halves of the deck. The bottom card on the top half of cards is the spectator's "chosen" card.

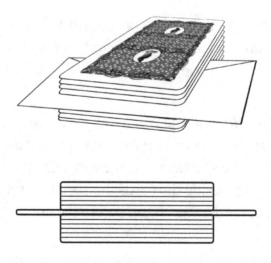

The Magic Number Book Test

Many methods can be used to conduct a book test. This method uses a "magic number." This is a forced number. The beauty of the magic number is that it can be used in a variety of ways, and it can be used in different magic tricks.

Effect: The magician shows the audience a book. He then asks a spectator to think of a random number and then do some basic math. Once the spectator has a total, the number is used to locate a page and a sentence in the book. The magician "reads the spectator's mind" and writes down his prediction. The spectator is asked to concentrate on the first word of the sentence. Even though the number was randomly selected, the magician correctly predicts the chosen word.

Setup: You will need a book with over 108 pages in it. A dictionary or a volume from the encyclopedia works well. Before you perform the trick, go to page 108 in the book. Go down to the ninth line. Remember what the first word is, as this will be your "prediction." The secret in this trick is that the number the spectator totals up will always be 1089. Try the trick with several different three-digit numbers, and you will see how it works. You will also see how this "magic number" can be used in a variety of magic tricks. You will need a pen and a small notepad of paper.

Performance: Show the book to the audience. Let them go through the book to see that all the pages are different. This will remove any doubt on whether the book is gimmicked.

Select a spectator from the audience. Give him a pen and a piece of paper. Tell the spectator, *"I would like you to write down any three-digit number. All the digits need to be different. Use digits between one and nine. Do not use the same digit twice. I will turn away so there is no way I will know which number you choose. Do not tell me what number you choose."* Turn away from the spectator and give him time to write down a three-digit number.

Now say, *"Good. I would like you to reverse the number that you chose, and write down the reversed number under the first number you wrote down."*

After this has been done, say, *"Now subtract the lesser number from the greater number. If your new number contains only two digits, put a zero in front of the number. Now reverse the number that you put the zero in front of, and then add the two numbers together. Do not tell me what the total is. If your new number contains three digits, then reverse that number and add the two numbers together."* (No matter what number the spectator originally chose, the total will always be 1089.)

Ask the spectator, *"How many digits are in your number?"* (Although you already know what the number is, you must build up the presentation.) Of course he will say four digits.

Now say, *"Please write down the first three digits of your number."* He will write down 108. Say, *"Now turn to the page that is represented by the number you just wrote down."* The spectator will turn to page 108 in the book.

Say, *"Now, go down to the line that is represented by your fourth number."* He will count down to the ninth line. Tell the spectator, *"I would like you to concentrate on the first word of that line."*

Look at the spectator as if you are concentrating on him. Say, *"I am going to attempt to read your mind."* Hold your fingertips up to your temples and close your eyes, as though you are trying to read the spectator's mind.

Write down on a piece of paper the word you remembered and know is the same as the spectator's word. Fold up the paper and put it down on the table. Ask the spectator, *"What is the word you are concentrating on?"* He will tell you his word. Say, *"Please open up the paper and read it aloud so everyone will know what I predicted by reading your mind."* The spectator will read your prediction and of course, it will be the same word as the one he was concentrating on. This is an effect the audience will remember for a long time!

Note: The magic number can be used in a variety of ways. Because you know the number will always be 1089, you can use it as a prediction in several different tricks. For example, you could use it in a magazine test. Just tell the spectator to go to page 10, line 8, and to count over nine words. I am sure you can think of many different ways to use the "magic number."

The Magic Number Book Test

This illustration shows how the spectator's three-digit number is added up. By using this method, the spectator's final number will always be 1089. Try it with your own numbers, and you will see how it works.

$$624$$
$$-426$$
$$=198$$

$$624$$
$$-426$$
$$=198$$
$$198$$
$$+891$$

$$624$$
$$-426$$
$$=198$$
$$198$$
$$+891$$
$$=1089$$

Super Mental Power Prediction

This is one of the quickest and easiest ways to make a prediction. It's a mentalism trick that you can perform anytime and anywhere.

Effect: A spectator shuffles a deck of cards. The magician goes through the deck and selects one card as his prediction. He places this card face down on the table. He then removes three other cards from the deck. The spectator chooses one of the three cards. The magician turns over his prediction card. It is the mate of the spectator's chosen card.

Setup: There is no setup required for this trick. It is self-working and can be done with a borrowed, shuffled deck.

Performance: Ask a spectator to shuffle the cards. Take the cards, spread them in your hands, and take out one of the Aces. Place it down on one side of the table. Say to the spectator, *"This is my prediction. I will place it here for the moment."*

Now go through the cards and take out any two cards (we will call these two cards the indifferent cards). Also take out another Ace. (If you took out the Ace of Spades for your prediction, take out the other black Ace the Ace of Clubs) Place the three cards down in front of the spectator. It is important for you to remember where the Ace is placed among the other two indifferent cards.

Say to the spectator, *"I would now like you to select any two cards. Do not look at them. Just pull them back toward you."*

Here's where the magic happens. If the spectator selects the two indifferent cards, you say, *"Out of the three cards, this is the card you left for me."* Turn it over to show the Ace. *"I predicted you would leave me the Ace."* Turn the other Ace over, and then turn over the two indifferent cards.

If the spectator takes one of the indifferent cards and the Ace say, *"I would now like you to select one of the cards."* If he selects the Ace tell him to turn it over.

Then you say, *"I predicted you would choose the Ace from the three cards."* Turn over your prediction Ace and then turn over the two indifferent cards on the table. If the spectator selects the indifferent card, then turn over the Ace and say, *"I predicted you would leave me the Ace out of the three cards."* Turn over the prediction Ace and the two indifferent cards.

As you can see, this is self-working and uses the Magician's Force, which is used in many other magic tricks.

Famous Forever

This is a fantastic mentalism effect! It is easy to do, and you will enjoy performing it. This is a great effect to entertain and amaze your audience.

Effect: The magician shows two sets of papers. Each set has four papers. The magician explains that the name of a famous president is written inside each of the folded papers. One set of papers is put into a paper bag and given to a spectator. The magician puts the other set of papers into another paper bag. The spectator is asked to reach into the bag and take out one of the folded papers. The magician also takes out one of the papers. The magician puts his paper on the table and then takes the paper the spectator is holding. The magician reads the name that is on the spectator's paper. The spectator then opens up the magician's paper. Amazingly, the names match! This is done again three times, and each time, the names match!

Setup: You will need two ordinary paper bags, such as paper lunch bags from any grocery store. You will also need eight pieces of blank computer paper. You will be making two identical sets of papers. Write the names of four famous presidents. I use Washington, Jefferson, Lincoln, and Kennedy, but you can use the names of ANY four people—for example, Elvis, Marilyn Monroe, Madonna, and Clint Eastwood. Or you can use the names of people who will be in your audience.

Write each name on one of the papers and fold it into fourths. (This is done by folding the paper in half from top to bottom, and then fold it side to side.) Just make sure the name cannot be seen through the folded paper. Put these papers in one of the paper bags.

Now make an identical set of papers. Write the names on the papers and fold them up.

Here is where the magic comes in. Do not do anything to the paper with Washington's name in it. Fold up one corner of the paper with Jefferson's name on it. (Fold only the top piece of paper in the corner.) Fold two corners of the paper with Lincoln's name in it. Fold three corners of the paper with Kennedy's name on it. In doing this, you will know by looking at them which name is inside the paper. (As a blind magician, I can feel the corners to let me know which name is written inside the paper.) Put this second set of papers in the other paper bag. You are now ready to perform this incredible magic trick!

Performance: Select a spectator from the audience. Say to the audience, *"I have two sets of identical papers. Each paper has the name of a president on it. The four presidents are Washington, Jefferson, Lincoln, and Kennedy."* Take the non-gimmicked set of papers and place it in one of the paper bags. Give it to the spectator to hold.

Say, *"I'll put the other set of papers in this bag."* Put the gimmicked papers in the other bag, and hold the bag in your left hand.

Tell the spectator, *"I would like you to reach inside your bag and take out one of the papers. Do not open it. Just place it on the table. I'll do the same thing."* Reach inside your bag and take out a paper. You will automatically know which name is on the paper you have by the folds in the paper. Place your paper on the table.

Pick up the spectator's folded paper. Tell the spectator to pick up your paper from *the table. Say, "Please open up the paper, but do not say what is written on it."* (You will already know what is written on the paper because of the folds.)

This is the important part: No matter what is written on the paper that you have, *say the name that you know is on the other paper.* For example, let's say you pull out Lincoln's paper (you will know this, as it has two folded-up corners). Set it down on the table. Let's say the spectator hands you the paper he took out of his bag, and it has Kennedy on it. When you read the name, just say Lincoln instead of Kennedy. It's as simple as that!

Fold the paper back up and set in down on the table. (Do not stack the papers or place them too close together.) Put one to the left side of the table and one to the right. This will prevent the spectator from connecting the names and figuring out the method.

Do this process three times. If, by luck, the spectator hands you the same name as the one you set down, then play it up for all it's worth—it will really seem miraculous to the spectator and the audience! Show the paper, and it will really seem like a mentalism miracle.

Gather up all the papers, and let the spectator look through them to see that there really are only two sets of papers. This is a great effect and if done properly, it can be a reputation maker!

Famous Forever

This illustration shows how to fold the corners on the different papers. By doing this, you will be able to identify each name simply by feeling the corners.

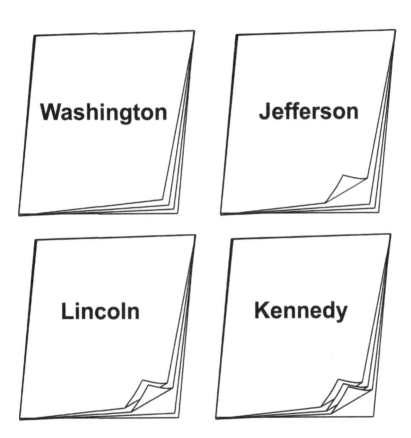

Magic with Ordinary Objects

Magic—Anytime, Anyplace, with Anything!

Magic with ordinary objects means just that. A magician should be able to do magic anytime and anyplace. I have done magic on the summit of Mount Kilimanjaro and on the floor of the ocean while surrounded by several sharks!

Ordinary objects can be anything from paper clips to rubber bands. Magic can be done with a pen, pencil, toothpicks, business cards, spoon, fork, salt shaker, coffee cup, napkins, etc. There really are no limits to what can be used in a magical way.

There are many books and videos on performing magic with ordinary objects. Of course, this type of magic is great for impromptu magic situations. Once you learn to do some magic with ordinary objects, you will always be ready to perform and entertain, anytime and anyplace!

George Gets Clipped!

This is one of my favorite pocket tricks. I always carry two paper clips so I can perform the trick. It has been around for a long time, but it is still a great trick. It is easy to do and can be done at anytime.

Effect: The magician borrows a dollar bill. He folds it and attaches a paper clip to it. He then folds it again and attaches another paper clip to the bill. He then grasps the ends of the bill and pulls out with both hands. Magically, the paper clips link together!

Setup: You will need two paper clips and a bill (the denomination does not matter, any bill will work). Fold the bill as shown in the illustration. Attach the paper clips as shown.

Performance: Borrow a dollar bill (you can actually use ANY bill). Fold the bill and attach the two paper clips. Grasp the ends of the bill and pull sharply and quickly outward, as indicated. The paper clips will link together!

George Gets Clipped!

The illustration on the left shows you how to attach the first paper clip. Fold the right side edge of the bill until it is in the middle of the seal (as shown). Attach the paper clip.

The illustration on the right shows how to fold the left side of the bill back toward the right side. Attach paper clip as shown.

George Gets Clipped!

The illustration below shows you how to grasp the dollar bill at the two ends. Pull in the direction of the arrows. The paper clips will link together automatically!

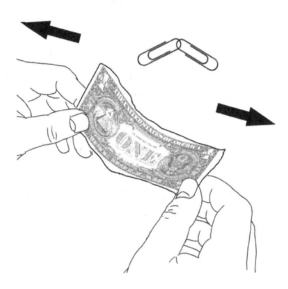

The Amazing Appearing Pencil

This is a nice mini-illusion. It is very visual and easy to do. It is a great way to magically produce a pencil for any other magic trick in which you use a pencil. For example, it would be a great way to produce the pencil for the It's in the Money trick described in this book.

Effect: The magician shows the audience a small drawer-type matchbox. He then proceeds to pull a full-length pencil from the box!

Setup: You will need a small drawer-type matchbox for this effect. These can be purchased at a drugstore or a grocery store. They are used for the small wooden safety matches—the box has a drawer that slides in and out.

To prepare the box, just cut out one end of the drawer. Then make a V-shaped space in the bottom cover of the box (the cover is the part that goes around the drawer). This is made to let the pencil slide into the box. The V-shaped space should be just big enough for the pencil to slide through easily. It is cut from both corners of one end of the cover. The tip of the V is in the center of the box (see illustration).

You will also need to wear a long-sleeved shirt or a jacket when performing this effect. Slide the pencil up your left sleeve before you do the trick.

Performance: Take the matchbox out of your pocket with your right hand. (Be sure not to expose the cutout part of the drawer or the V-shaped space in the bottom of the box.) Put the matchbox in the palm of your left hand. As you do this, bend your left hand back and use your right fingers to grasp the tip of the pencil.

Slide the matchbook back so the pencil slides into the V-space on the bottom cover.

Now simply reach inside the matchbox with your right thumb and index finger, and pull out the pencil. This will be startling to your audience!

The Amazing Appearing Pencil

This illustration shows you how to place the pencil in your sleeve (as shown by the dotted line). Simply open the matchbox, grasp the pencil, and pull it out through the holes in the box. The other illustrations show how to cut the matchbox.

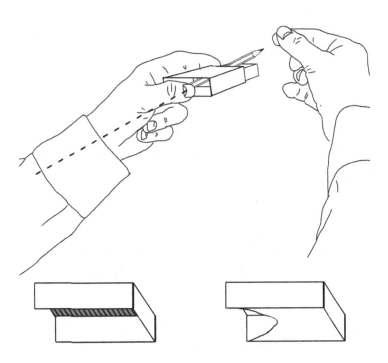

Let's Do the Twist!

What can be more impromptu than performing magic with two ordinary straws? Once you learn this trick, you will have an effect you can perform anywhere at any time. This is a great trick for magicians who perform in restaurants.

Effect: The magician passes out two ordinary drinking straws. He then twists them together, not once but twice. He then is able to pull the straws apart!

Setup: There is no setup required for this trick. You will need two ordinary drinking straws.

Performance: Pass out the straws so they can be examined by the audience. Take one straw in each hand. Hold the straw in your left hand horizontally. Hold the straw in your right hand vertically. Place the vertical straw behind the horizontal straw so they touch in the middle.

Pull down the top of the vertical straw toward you and wrap it around the horizontal straw. Wrap it around so the top of the straw goes back to the top. Hold both straws together in the middle with your left thumb and index finger.

Now wrap the right end of the horizontal straw back toward you. Wrap it around the vertical straw until the right end is back to the right-hand side. Once again, press the straws together with your left thumb and index finger.

Now bring the left end of the horizontal straw toward you and over to the right end of the straw. Hold both ends together with your right hand. Bring the top end of the vertical straw and the bottom end of the vertical straw together in your left hand.

Blow on the straws (this is to make the presentation look more dramatic). Now pull both hands apart. The straws will seem to magically pop right through each other!

Let's Do the Twist!

This is a very easy trick. (I hope the illustrations will help to explain how to fold the straws around each other.) After you practice it a few times, you will be able to do it quickly and easily. For illustration purposes, one straw is dark and one is light, but the trick can be done with any color and type of straw.

The illustration on the left shows how to wrap the dark straw around the light straw. It is wrapped by pulling the top of the dark straw around the middle of the light straw.

The illustration on the right shows how to wrap the light straw around the dark straw. Grasp the right end of the light straw and bring it toward you. While you are doing this, hold the straws together with your left thumb and index finger.

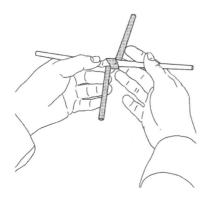 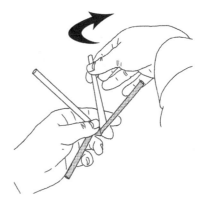

Let's Do the Twist!

The illustration on the left shows how to continue wrapping the light straw around the dark straw. The right side of the light straw is brought toward you and wrapped completely around the dark straw.

The illustration on the right shows how to grasp the straws. Bend the dark straw toward you, and bring it to the other end of the straw. Hold these two ends with your left hand. Now grasp the left side of the light straw, and fold it toward you and to the right side of the straw. Hold these two ends with your right hand.

Pull the straws apart as shown by the arrows.

The Impossible Pencil Penetration

This is a very visual trick. It will add a nice variety to any close-up magic routine. It is simple to do. You will enjoy performing this effect.

Effect: The magician shows a rubber band, a business card, and a pencil. He places the rubber band around the card so that it is held by two opposite corners. He then pushes a pencil through the middle of the card and in doing so, it goes inside the rubber band. The magician asks a spectator to hold both ends of the pencil. Amazingly, the magician causes the rubber band to penetrate the pencil! He hands everything out for examination by the audience.

Setup: You will need a pencil, a rubber band, and a business card. This is a great way to pass out your business card. You can have some cards printed up that have space in the center where the pencil goes through.

Performance: Pass out the rubber band, pencil, and business card for examination. Take them back, and place the rubber band around two opposite corners on the business card. Hold the card in your right hand. As you reach for the pencil (which is in your left pants pocket), simply use your right thumb to slide the rubber band past the center of the card (see illustration). As this is done behind the card, it is concealed from view of the audience.

Take the pencil, and push it through the center of the card. The audience will assume the pencil also has gone through the inside of the rubber band. However, because you have pushed the rubber band past the center, the rubber band is already on the *OUTSIDE* of the pencil.

Ask a spectator to hold both ends of the pencil. Tell the spectator you would like to remove the rubber band without tearing the business card. Go through the motions of doing just that. Then say, *"Please watch closely."* Pull the rubber band off the card. As you do, the rubber band will seem to pass through the pencil! The audience will be amazed by this magical penetration.

The Impossible Pencil Penetration

The illustration on the left shows how the rubber band is put on the business card. The dotted lines show where the rubber band is on the back of the card.

The illustration on the right shows you how to move the rubber band with your thumb. This move is concealed from the audience by the card.

This illustration shows the pencil pushed through the card. Now, just pull the rubber band off the card. It will appear to the audience that the rubber band has magically penetrated the pencil!

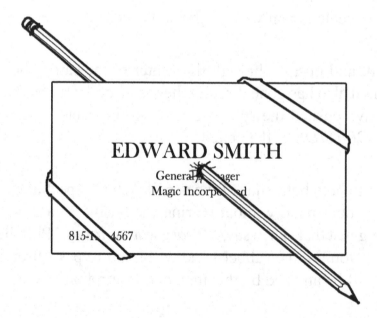

Super-Straw

This is a great effect for any table magic routine. It is fun because it uses audience participation.

Effect: The magician hands out several ordinary drinking straws to the audience. He then takes a straw and places it through the handle of a cup. He grasps both ends of the straw and then proceeds to lift the cup. Amazingly, the straw remains straight. Then the magician lets go of one end of the straw. The straw does not bend! The audience tries to do this but finds that their straws bend from the weight of the cup. If they let go of one end, the cup will fall to the table.

Setup: The secret to this magic trick is simplicity itself. All you need is a strong wire that is cut a little shorter than the straw. Just cut a section of a coat hanger that is about a half-inch shorter than the straw. Place the wire in the straw—now you are ready to perform this trick. Make sure that you use a straw in which the wire cannot be seen.

Note: I use straws that are sealed in paper. I carefully open the paper at one end. I remove the straw, insert the wire, and put the straw back in the paper. All you need to do is hold your thumb and index finger over the opening in the paper. By doing this, the paper around the straw still will seem sealed, and you will help remove any suspicion that the straw is gimmicked.

Performance: Make sure you know which straw has the wire in it. Then pass out several of the other straws to the audience.

Take the paper cover off your straw, and place the straw through the handle of a cup (a coffee cup works well).

Grasp both ends of the straw—make sure you grasp both ends of the wire that is concealed inside the straw. Ask the audience to watch carefully. Very slowly pick up the cup. Lift it off the table (the wire will support the cup). Tell the audience, *"Of course, the trick is to hypnotize the straw."* Pause for a moment, and then let go of one end of the straw. Make sure you are gripping the wire tightly so the straw remains horizontal. You'll need to have an index finger under the straw to securely hold the straw and wire level. The audience will be amazed.

Say, *"Go ahead and give it a try."* While the audience is trying to support their cups with their straws, grasp the free end of the straw and slowly lower your cup to the table. Now just bring the straw back to the edge of the table. Turn the straw vertical, and let the wire slide out of the straw and into your lap. You will have plenty of misdirection to do this, as the audience will be trying to support their cups with their straws. Put the wire away at your convenience.

Super-Straw

The illustration below shows the magician holding the straw in his left hand and the wire in his right hand. Of course, the wire is held below the table and out of view of the audience.

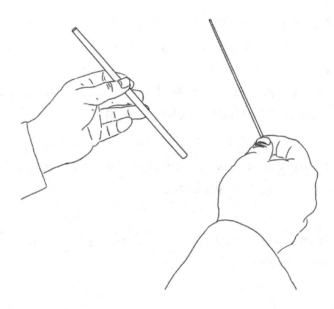

Super-Straw

The illustration below shows how the wire is inserted into the straw. The wire is represented by the dotted line. This move is done below the table and out of the view of the audience.

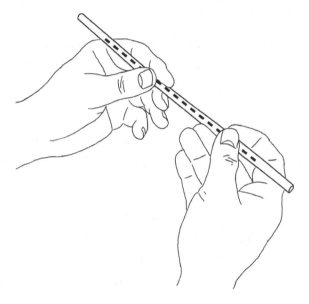

This illustration shows how the trick looks to the audience. The straw is held by both ends. It appears to the audience that the straw does not bend from the weight of the cup!

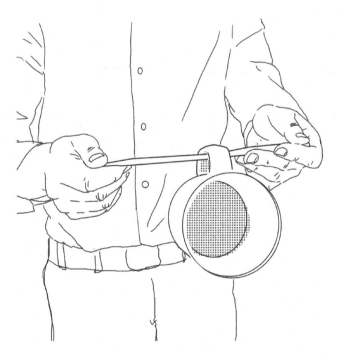

Pin Penetration

This trick has been around for many years. I have found it in just about every beginner's magic book. It's a great pocket trick that you will be able to carry with you anywhere.

Effect: The magician shows the audience two ordinary safety pins. He links them together and then, in a blink of an eye, he pulls them apart. The pins are still locked!

Setup: You will need two ordinary safety pins. The larger the safety pin, the easier it is to work with. I use 2-inch basting pins that I bought at a fabric store.

Performance: Pass the safety pins so they may be examined by the audience. When they are returned, open one of the safety pins and link it through the other pin. (You must link them in this way: The opening bar of the pin in your right hand must be to the right. The opening bar of the pin in your left hand must be at the bottom. See illustration.)

Hold the pins so they form an X. Grasp both smaller ends of the pins. Twist the pin in your right hand away from you. At the same time, twist the pin in your left hand back toward you.

Quickly pull your hands apart. The pins will separate without opening!

This effect is well worth the time it takes to practice it. You will be able to carry this all-time classic pocket trick with you wherever you go.

Pin Penetration

The illustration below shows how the pins are linked together. The opening bar of one pin is on the bottom. The other pin is inserted through the closed pin, as shown.

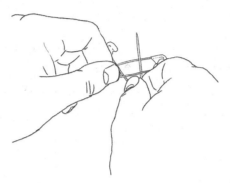

This illustration shows how the two pins are locked together to form a X. Twist the pin in the left hand out, and twist the pin in the right hand toward you.

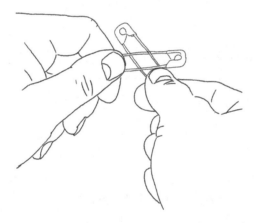

Quickly pull the pins apart by pulling in the direction shown by the arrows. The pins will separate while they are both still locked!

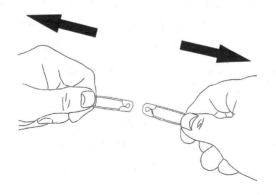

Jumping Rubber Band

This is one of the first tricks I ever learned—it probably is the first trick that many beginning magicians learn. It is a classic impromptu magic trick. There are actually several effects that can be done with rubber bands.

This is an example of the type of tricks that are taught in David Copperfield's Project Magic. Physical therapists use this trick to help motivate patients in the rehabilitation process. This particular trick is used to increase strength in the fingers and also to improve the circulation in the hands. Magic is a fun way to get patients involved in physical therapy.

Effect: The magician shows a rubber band and places it over the index finger and middle finger of his right hand. He then closes his hand into a fist. He quickly opens his hand and magically, the rubber band has jumped over to his ring finger and little finger!

Setup: No setup is required for this trick. You will need a rubber band. The rubber band should fit snugly around the fingers, but it must not be too tight. After practicing the trick a time or two, you will be able to determine the size of rubber band that works for you.

Performance: Show the audience the rubber band, and place it around the index and middle fingers of your right hand. Show the front, back, and side of your hand. Now hold your palm toward you. Pull on the rubber band with your left fingers as if you are testing the tension. Do this a couple of times.

As you pull back the rubber band for the third time, turn your hand down, and close your hand into a fist. As you do this, simply insert *ALL* your fingers into the rubber band. (The audience will not be able to see this, as your hand will be down.) The rubber band should now be around your fingertips.

Say to the audience, *"Please watch closely."* Snap the fingers of your left hand. Quickly straighten out the fingers of your right hand. The rubber band will automatically jump over your ring and little fingers!

Jumping Rubber Bands

The illustration on the left shows you how to place the rubber band over the index and middle fingers of your right hand. The thumb, ring finger, and little finger are held together. The left hand is pulling on the rubber band.

The illustration on the right shows the palm of the right hand and shows how to slip the rubber band over the ring and little fingers. Do this after pulling the rubber band a couple of times and while making a fist.

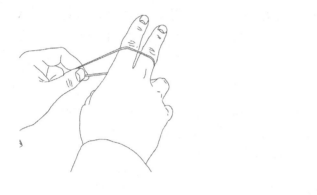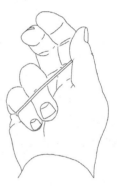

This illustration shows the end of the trick, after the rubber band has "magically" jumped from the index and middle fingers to the ring and little fingers. The right hand is open with the palm facing down.

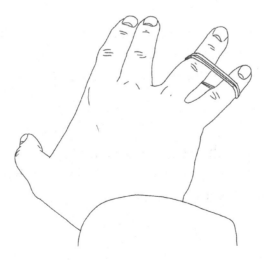

Cut and Restored String

This is an easy to do impromptu magic trick. It is fun to perform, and your audience will be amazed.

Effect: The magician threads a string through an ordinary drinking straw. He then bends the straw in half and cuts the straw and string in half. He then magically restores the string!

Setup: For this trick you must prepare an ordinary drinking straw. Just cut a slot in the straw about four inches long. This slot is in the center of the straw. You will also need a string about eighteen inches long. A shoestring works well with this trick. You will need a pair of scissors.

Performance: Show the audience a straw and string (be careful not to expose the slot in the straw). Let a spectator pull on both ends of the string. This will remove any suspicion that the string is gimmicked.

Say, *"Watch as I thread the string through the straw."* Thread the string through the straw, making sure that the slot in the straw is on the bottom. Bend the straw in half. Pull down on the ends of the string that are hanging out the ends of the straw. When you do this, the string will drop down a few inches out of the slot in the straw. This is concealed by your left hand.

Say, *"I will now cut the straw and the string in two."* Take the scissors in your right hand and cut the straw. (The audience will assume the string is still inside the straw, but it is concealed behind your left hand.)

Now say, *"I will now magically restore the string."* Keep the middle of the string covered with your right hand. Make a motion over the string, as if you are magically restoring it. Grasp the string with your left hand, and pull the string from side to side to show that it has been restored!

Cut and Restored String

The illustration below shows how to cut a slot in the straw. The slot should be big enough for the string to drop out of it when the straw is folded.

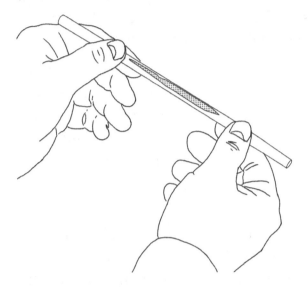

This illustration shows how to conceal the string when the straw is folded. The hand completely covers the string from the view of the audience. After you cut the straw, simply pull on one end of the string to show how it has been "restored."

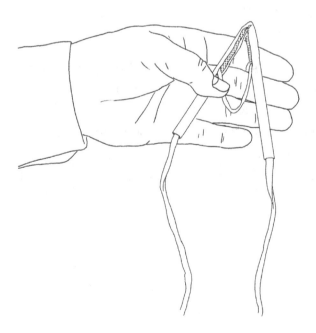

The Impossible Glass-on-Plate Effect!

This trick will add some variety to your table magic routine. It is quite easy to do and is very visual. It is an impromptu trick that plays big.

Effect: The magician shows a glass and a plate to the audience. He then attempts to balance the glass on the edge of the plate. Although it seems impossible, the magician finally balances the glass on the plate!

Setup: For this trick you will need a dinner plate and a glass. A wine glass looks best, but you can do it with just about any type of glass, such as a water glass or a glass tumbler. I have actually done this effect with a paper plate and a paper cup. After you practice the trick a few times, I am sure you will find different variations for the trick.

Performance: Show the audience the glass and the plate. Grasp the plate with your right hand. Hold the plate vertically, with the face of the plate toward the audience. It should be held so that the right thumb can reach just below the top edge of the plate (see illustration).

Slowly set the glass on top of the plate. Immediately lift it off. Set it back down as if you are trying to find the balance point of the glass. Do this two times.

On the third time, set the glass slightly toward you so that only the front of the glass sits on the edge of the plate. Extend your thumb so the glass can rest on it. (This will be hidden from the audience by the plate.) The glass will be supported by the plate and your thumb. Hold the plate and glass steady. LEAVE THE GLASS BALANCED ON THE PLATE FOR ONLY A FEW SECONDS—any longer will draw too much suspicion. Lift the glass off, and set it down on the table.

The Impossible Glass-on-Plate Effect!

The illustration on the left shows the magician attempting to place the glass on the plate.

The illustration on the right shows how the glass is placed on top of the plate. The position of the right thumb is concealed from the audience view by the plate.

The illustration on the left is a side view, showing how to hold the plate.

The illustration on the right shows a view from the back of the plate. It shows how to balance the glass with your thumb.

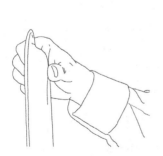 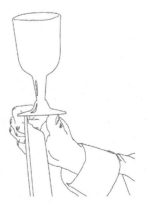

Torn and Restored Napkin

This is one of my favorite tricks and is one of the first magic tricks I learned. It can be done anywhere and anytime. Although it is simple to do, it plays big. I have done this trick in many different countries and for all ages of people. I am sure you will love performing this trick as much as I do.

Effect: The magician says he would like to teach the audience a trick and will explain how it is done. He takes a napkin and rolls it up into a ball. He then shows how he secretly palms the napkin in his left hand. He then takes an identical napkin and tears it up into several pieces. The magician then shows how he switches the torn pieces for the secret whole napkin. He opens up the hidden napkin to show that the torn napkin has been restored. The audience thinks that they now know how the trick is done. The magician tells the audience that when they do the trick, it is important not to expose the torn pieces of napkin.

Then the magician says that *IF* that should happen, they would *REALLY* need to restore the torn pieces of napkin. Amazingly, the magician opens the torn pieces of napkin to show that the pieces of napkin *REALLY* have been restored! Only then does the audience realize that they really did not learn the secret to this delightful magic trick.

Setup: You will need three identical paper napkins. I use three plain white napkins. (You can also get some napkins at your favorite restaurant. Take three extra napkins with you. Some restaurants have their logo on the napkin. This really makes for consistency in the effect.) You can also use three Kleenex tissues for this trick. I would recommend beginning with tissues, as it is really easy to conceal, especially if you have small hands.

Unfold one napkin, opening it all the way up. For instructional purposes, we will call this napkin 1. Lay it down on a table. Unfold another napkin and lay directly on top of napkin 1. This second one will be called napkin 2.

Take the third napkin (napkin 3), and crumple it up into a small ball. Place this napkin ball (napkin 3) at the bottom center of napkins 1 and 2. Now roll the napkins, down from the top, into a tube. Roll the two napkins so that the "napkin ball" (napkin 3) is inside the tube. The napkin ball will be at the bottom edge, with the tube rolled around it.

Also, place a pen in your right pants pocket to use as a magic wand later in the trick. You are now ready to perform this trick.

While the instructions on how to perform this trick may seem lengthy, I will break it down to make it easier to learn. The trick only takes a few minutes to perform.

Performance: Pick up the tube with your right hand. Grab it in the middle so you can hold the napkin ball inside the other two napkins. The bottom edges of napkins 1 and 2 should be up against the palm of your right hand. (This will make it very easy to just curl your right fingers around the napkin ball when you open up the napkins to show the audience.)

Say to the audience, *"I would like to teach you a magic trick, but you must promise not to tell how it is done."* Start to unroll the napkins. When you get to the bottom end of the tube, curl your right fingers around the napkin ball to conceal it. (Curl your right little finger, ring finger, and middle finger around the napkin ball.) Make sure it stays hidden from the audience's view. Practice holding the crumpled napkin ball under your curled fingers. Make sure you do this naturally and without calling attention to it. You should be very relaxed during this routine.

Separate the two whole napkins (1 and 2). Hold one in your left hand and the other in your right hand. (Your right hand will also be concealing the napkin 3, so make sure you do not expose the hidden napkin.)

Say to the audience, *"One of these napkins is going to be a secret napkin. It will be concealed in your left hand."* Take the napkin 2 (in your left hand) and crumple it up into a small ball. Now, actually show the audience how they should curl their left fingers around the napkin ball to conceal it. (This is exactly what you are doing with the napkin 3 in your right hand, but your audience does not know this.)

Say to the audience, *"Notice that the napkin is concealed from the view of the audience. This is the secret to the trick. Of course, this is done before you start the trick."*

Then tell the audience, *"This is what you should say to YOUR audience: 'You are going to begin the trick by tearing up a napkin.'"* And that is just what you do. Tear napkin 1, which is in your right hand, into several pieces.

Say to the audience, *"Now you must roll the torn pieces of napkin into a small ball."* That is what you do—roll the pieces of napkin into a ball. Now hold the napkin ball between the thumbs and index fingers of both hands.

Separate your hands and hold the torn pieces of napkin 1 in your right fingertips. Say to the audience, *"Now this is what you have. You have a torn napkin, rolled up in a ball, in your right hand, and the secret whole napkin (napkin 2) curled up in your left hand."* At this time the audience will think you are letting them in on a secret.

Bring your left thumb and index finger over to your right thumb and index finger (which is holding the torn napkin 2). Do this as though you are tightening up the torn pieces of napkin to make them more compact.

Here is the real secret of the trick: As you do this, roll the torn pieces of napkin 2 behind whole napkin 3. Just move the small torn pieces downward and behind the whole napkin. Then curl your fingers around the torn pieces of napkin so it is concealed from the audience. Do this naturally and smoothly, so it looks like all you are doing is compacting the torn pieces. However, you will now have the whole napkin 3 at your right fingertips, and the torn pieces (napkin 2) will be behind it.

You will now be able to open up your right hand. It will appear that the torn napkin is still at your fingertips (actually, the torn pieces are behind the whole napkin). Doing this will show that your right hand is empty—and that it has been empty all along. This will eliminate any suspicion by the audience that a napkin was concealed in your right hand (even though this was exactly what you were doing). Say to the audience, *"You can show YOUR audience the torn-up pieces of the napkin."*

Take whole napkin 3 from your right thumb and index finger, grasping it with your left thumb and index finger. (Remember that the audience will think you are putting the torn pieces of napkin in your left hand.)

Say to the audience, *"Of course, to do magic you need a magic wand. You can use a pen as a magic wand."* Reach into your right pants pocket to take out the pen. As you do this, open your fingers and dump the torn pieces of the napkin. Take the pen from your pocket. (Practice this move, as it should be one continuous motion. Do not hesitate when grasping the pen or let the torn pieces of napkin fall out of your hand. The audience should not know that you are dumping the torn pieces in your pocket.) The movement of reaching for your magic wand is natural and seems logical. This will provide cover for what you are really doing.

At this point you will have the pen in your right hand. You will be holding a napkin ball with your left thumb and index finger (the audience will assume this is the torn pieces of napkin). You will have a whole napkin concealed with the fingers of your left hand.

Say to the audience, *"Here's where the real magic comes in. The real reason for reaching for the magic wand is to direct attention away from your left hand. You do this so you can switch the torn-up pieces with the whole napkin that is hidden behind your fingers. Here, let me show you how it is done."* Show the audience your left hand, as though you are showing them the secret to the trick. Say, *"Take the pieces of the torn napkin and push them down with your left thumb. Roll them down and behind the whole napkin. Then just curl your fingers around the torn pieces of napkin to conceal it. Roll the whole napkin to the tips of your thumb and index finger."* Show the audience this openly and slowly. Tell them that this is done while you are reaching for your magic wand.

Say to the audience, *"All you need to do now is just wave your magic wand over your left hand."* Put the pen back into your pocket. (I hold the pen with my right thumb and index finger when waving the wand. This shows that your right hand is empty and that nothing is concealed in it).

Say, "*Now all you have to do is open the whole napkin, and your audience will be amazed as they think you really restored a torn napkin.*" Open up the whole napkin and show the audience.

Here's the kicker: Say to the audience, "*Of course, when you show the whole napkin, you must be very careful not to show any of the pieces of the torn napkin that is concealed behind your fingers. Because if you do this it would expose how the trick is done.*" Then say, "*However, if that does happen, there is something you can do—you must actually restore the torn pieces of napkin!*" And with that, open up the concealed napkin to show that it is a whole napkin. (Remember that this is the napkin that the audience thinks is the torn pieces of the napkin.)

Your audience will really be amazed by this trick. They thought they knew the secret to the trick, but they will realize that you actually have done something magical!

Pick up the other full napkin so you have a whole napkin in both hands. Turn them so the audience can see both sides. Lay the napkins down, snap your fingers on both hands, and turn your palms toward the audience so they can see that your hands are empty.

Practice this trick, and you will have a magical effect that you will love to perform!

Torn and Restored Napkin

The illustration on the left shows how to prepare the napkins to begin the trick. One of the full napkins is laid directly on top of the other. The "napkin ball" is placed where shown by the dotted lines.

The illustration on the right shows how to hold the rolled-up napkins in your left hand. The napkin ball is inside and is held in place by your left thumb.

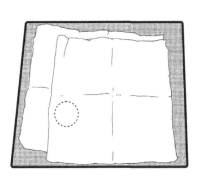 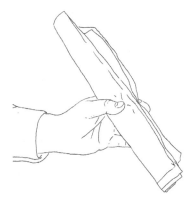

The illustration below shows how the napkin ball drops into the right hand when the napkins are placed in the right hand. As you start to unroll the full napkins, just grasp the napkin ball and conceal it with the middle, ring, and little fingers of the right hand.

Torn and Restored Napkin

The illustration below shows how a "napkin ball" is concealed in each hand. While the audience is aware of the concealed napkin ball in your left hand, they are not aware that there is also a napkin ball concealed in your right hand. Now the remaining full napkin is torn in two, as shown. The two torn pieces are put together, torn many times, and then rolled up into a ball.

This is a detailed illustration of how the torn pieces (which have been rolled into a ball) are at the fingertips of the right hand. The original napkin ball is concealed with the middle, ring, and little fingers of the right hand. To switch the torn napkin for the full napkin, just push the torn napkin back and under the original napkin ball, and then use your fingertips to pull the original napkin ball forward.

Project Magic

There are many wonderful aspects to magic. Not only can magic be used to entertain people, but it also can be used to help people, physically, mentally, and emotionally.

Project Magic was created by David Copperfield. It is a program designed to use magic to help in the rehabilitation process of patients with physical limitations. Magicians work with occupational and physical therapists to teach magic to the hospital patients. The magic tricks used in Project Magic were developed to improve many aspects of a patient's rehabilitation. Learning the tricks certainly helps with cognitive and spatial relationship skills. Sleight-of-hand tricks can help with coordination and dexterity. As a blind magician, magic has helped me in many areas of my life. It can certainly help anyone with a disability to improve his or her self-confidence. I know for a fact that magic can help promote a positive self-image and help to build self-esteem—because it has done so for me. Anyone with a disability could be helped by Project Magic.

Project Magic was first started in February 1982. I heard about the program and was fortunate to meet David at a magicians convention in Las Vegas. He encouraged me, and I soon began teaching magic to occupational and physical therapists at local hospitals. It was very successful, and many patients were helped by learning magic. The therapists told me that magic helped to motivate the patients in their rehabilitation. It really helps patients who are depressed because of their disability.

The program was first started in the Daniel Freeman Memorial Hospital in Inglewood, California. It has since spread to hospitals around the world.

I have always said that *real* magic is the ability to touch the lives of others in a positive way. With that in mind, David Copperfield is not only one of the greatest magicians in the world. He also is certainly one of the greatest human beings in the world. His creation, Project Magic, has helped so many people by bringing magic into their lives.

Famous Magicians

There are many famous magicians in the world. Many people are familiar with names like Houdini, Blackstone, Henning, and Copperfield. The history of magic is so interesting because of the personalities of great magicians. The following is a list of famous magicians with whom I am familiar. If famous magicians are not on this list, it is not because they are not as famous as those on the list. It only means that I have no personal knowledge of them. I certainly apologize for any magician of fame who is not listed. There are so many who have made magic what it is. I have a deep respect for those who have enhanced the art of magic.

Criss Angel (Christopher Nicholas Sarantakos, American magician, b. 1967). Criss Angel is a magician, an illusionist, and an escapologist. He is probably best known for his TV show, *Mindfreak*. He is also known for his show at the Luxor in Las Vegas.

Carl Ballantine (Meyer Kessler, American magician and actor, b. 1922). Carl Ballantine is probably best known for his part as Gruber in *McHale's Navy*. To many, however, he is best known for his contribution to comedy magic. He was known as Ballantine the Great, and his act consisted of doing magic that did not always go right. I remember his act from watching him on the *Ed Sullivan Show* in the late 1950s and early 1960s.

Henry Black (American magician, b.1962). Henry Black is a well-known magician who performs both close-up and stage magic. Henry has entertained audiences of all ages and for all occasions. One of Henry's special talents is his ability to make his own props. He has made some excellent props from wood, such as the classic Chop Cup. Henry has made everything from his own guillotine illusion to high-quality bunny boxes and tip-over illusions. His craftsmanship is outstanding. One of his most interesting projects was to build a tip-over illusion that had to be big enough to produce Santa Claus for a Christmas show!

Harry Blackstone Jr. (American magician, 1934–1997). Harry Blackstone Jr. was the son of the famous stage magician Harry Blackstone Sr. Harry carried on the tradition of his father and performed many of the same illusions. He was a very nice person. I met Harry in a Baskin-Robbins ice cream shop in Honolulu, Hawaii. I was there to attend the International Brotherhood of Magicians convention, and Harry was there to perform for the attendees at the convention. We talked about magic and some of the other acts at the convention. What a great person, both on and off stage.

Harry Blackstone Sr. (American magician, 1885–1965). Harry Blackstone Sr. was one of the greatest magicians of all time. He had a large traveling illusion show and was famous throughout the world.

David Blaine (David Blaine White, American magician, b. 1973). David Blaine is probably best known for his street-magic performances in his television specials. He has received worldwide attention for his record-breaking feats of endurance. Among his many accomplishments are his being buried alive for over seven days! He was also enclosed in a huge block of ice for over sixty-three hours. One of his most incredible feats was being submerged in a water-filled sphere, where he stayed for over seven days. He is very much like a modern-day Houdini.

Eugene Burger (American magician, b. 1939). Eugene Burger not only performs magic, but he also is known as a philosopher of magic. He teaches others how to be more creative with their magic routines. Eugene is probably best known for his excellent close-up magic and mentalism, in which he combines storytelling and superb magic technique. What makes the magic so unique is Eugene's presentation of magic, which makes it so entertaining for the audience. Eugene is also a fantastic teacher of magic and frequently teaches with Jeff McBride at the Magic and Mystery School in Las Vegas.

Lance Burton (William Lance Burton, American magician, b. 1960). Lance Burton is a well-known stage magician who has his own show at the Monte Carlo Resort in Las Vegas, Nevada. I was at his show in February 2006, and it was fantastic! Lance has made many television appearances. I remember when Lance did his dove act on the *Tonight Show* (hosted by Johnny Carson). I met Lance during a magicians convention. He is one of the friendliest people you will ever meet. It is no wonder that his stage show is one of the biggest draws in Vegas.

Cardini (Richard Valentine Pitchford, Welsh magician, 1894–1973). Cardini, as the name implies, was known for his excellent card manipulation and sleight of hand. In 1999 *Magic* magazine named Cardini one of *Magic* magazine's Top Magicians of the Twentieth Century.

Robert "Big Bob" Coleman (American magician, b. 1955). Robert "Big Bob" Coleman is also known as Bilbo the Clown. He has performed everything from kids shows to large stage shows. He is well known for his expertise with balloons and has created four videos on the subject. He also has a video on balloon magic that is very popular. Bob created many of the effects he performs in his act. Bob is excellent at restaurant magic and is a big hit as he combines his talent of his balloon creations with his fantastic close-up magic.

David Copperfield (David Seth Kotkin, American magician, b. 1956). Much like the name Houdini, Copperfield is the name that is mentioned when people talk of famous magicians. Simply put, David Copperfield is the most successful magician of all time. Most people are familiar with David Copperfield from his *The Magic of David Copperfield* television specials. He also has entertained thousands with his traveling stage show. Some of his most famous illusions have been making the Statue of Liberty disappear and walking through the Great Wall of China! I wrote to David in 1982 to become involved in his Project Magic. I later met David at a magicians convention in Las Vegas. He encouraged me to get involved in the program. Project Magic is a program of using magic to help disabled patients in the rehabilitation process. David is one of the highest paid celebrities in the world and has received a star on the well-known Hollywood Walk of Fame. He is also one of the nicest people I have ever met. He has inspired me, as well as many other magicians. He also inspired me to use magic to help other people, especially those who might be facing adversity or who have limitations.

Dante (Harry August Jansen, American magician, 1883–1955). Although Dante was born in Denmark, he immigrated to the United States when he was six years old. He began magic at an early age and at one time built illusions for the legendary magician Howard Thurston. He is famous for using the phrase "Sim Sala Bim." Dante can be seen saying this phrase in the movie *A Hunting We Will Go*, which starred the comedy legends Laurel & Hardy. Dante was one of the last of the Golden Age of Magic performers.

T. Nelson Downs (Thomas Nelson Downs, American magician, 1867–1938). T. Nelson Downs was well known for his expertise with coin manipulation. He was so good that he was known as the "King of Koins." It is interesting that T. Nelson Downs never took any magic lessons. His tricks were self-taught, and he mastered them very well. One of his most famous effects was the Miser's Dream. In this trick, a performer produces several coins from thin air. Many magicians, including me, still perform the Miser's Dream routine in stage shows. Downs also wrote several magic books. His first book, which was published in 1900, was *Modern Coin Manipulation.* You might find it interesting that I used *Modern Coin Manipulation* as a reference for some of the coin magic in this book.

Joseph Dunninger (American magician and mentalist, 1892–1975). Joseph Dunninger was best known for his amazing mentalism performances. He amazed audiences on the radio in the 1940s and then on television in the 1950s and 1960s. It is interesting to note that both President Theodore "Teddy" Roosevelt and the famous inventor Thomas Edison were big fans of Dunninger. Dunninger was also a good friend of Harry Houdini's.

Dan Eppard (American magician, b. 1974). Dan Eppard is well known for his innovative close-up and stage magic. He has a great stand-up comedy magic routine. I like Dan's magic, as he puts comedy into a lot of his effects, and it makes it very entertaining. Dan has performed magic in a wide variety of settings, including kids shows, colleges, banquets, restaurants, bars and many different special events. Dan has a great Chop Cup routine that is amazing. Dan is also well known for his mind-blowing mentalism effects. He has even built calculators that he uses in some of his fantastic mental magic effects.

John Gaughan (American illusion designer and manufacturer, b. 1940). John Gaughan is a creator and builder of magic illusions. He creates illusions for the best magicians in the world, including David Copperfield, Criss Angel, David Blaine, and many more. His illusions are works of art. His craftsmanship and technical expertise combine to produce some of the most beautiful illusions in the world. I wanted to include him in this list of famous magicians, as he makes the magic happen. John Gaughan is truly famous for his contribution to magic. As a blind magician, I only wish I could see one of Mr. Gaughan's creations. I am sure it would be something like an art student who gets the opportunity to see the Mona Lisa.

Rich "Riverboat Rich" Gough (American magician, b. 1944). Rich Gough is well known as a teacher of magic. He has taught countless magicians, including me, the art of close-up and stage magic. Many of the magicians Rich has taught have become full-time professionals. Like many magicians, I began taking card magic classes from Rich several years ago. He was not overwhelmed by the fact that I was blind. In fact, he saw it as a challenge. Instead of telling me what I couldn't do in magic, Rich found ways to overcome any problems I encountered. Along with my close-up magic, Rich also taught me my stage magic, including my dove routine and other classic magic effects, such as the Zombie routine, and manipulations with canes, candles, and billiard balls, as well as stage illusions.

The Amazing Haundini (Gary Haun, American magician, b. 1952). The Amazing Haundini has entertained audiences throughout the world. Although blind, the Amazing Haundini is one of only a few magicians in the world to perform magic before a live national television audience (*Rosie O'Donnell Show,* 2000) and in a full-length theatrical film *(Jane's Journey,* 2010). The Amazing Haundini is also one of the few magicians in the world to have performed magic on his way to the summit of Mt. Kilimanjaro in Africa and also while shark diving off the coast of the Bahamas. Gary is the first blind magician to receive the Doctor of Magic degree from the Magic Academy of the International Magicians Society.

Doug Henning (Douglas James Henning, Canadian magician, 1947–2000). Doug Henning was a magician, illusionist, and escape artist and was famous for his many television appearances in the 1970s. After performing in his very successful Broadway show, *Spellbound,* Henning brought magic to television. *Doug Henning's World of Magic* first appeared in 1975.

Alexander Herrmann (French magician, 1844–1896). Alexander Herrmann was known as Herrmann the Great and was one of the greatest magicians of all time. He had quite an interesting life. If you like reading biographies of famous magicians, I would highly recommend you begin with Alexander Hermann.

Brian Holt (American magician, b. 1966). Brian Holt performs all types of magic for audiences of all ages. He performs both close-up and stage magic and can entertain audiences, whether it is one person or thousands of people. Brian began magic at the early age of seven. His interest in magic began when he read a book about simple magic tricks in elementary school. (Author's note: I can only hope that *THIS* book will inspire someone to be interested in magic and possibly one day become a fantastic magician like Brian.) Brian is well known for his stage magic, in which he performs many of magic's classic illusions. He performs at many different events, including schools, fairs, banquets, and other large events. He has a great stand-up comedy routine. Brian is also known for his extensive knowledge of magic and is always willing to help other magicians.

Robert-Houdin (Jean Eugene Robert-Houdin, French magician, 1805–1871). Robert Houdin is considered by many people to be the father of modern magic. It is interesting to know that the famous magician Harry Houdini adapted his name from Robert Houdin as a way to honor the great magician.

Harry Houdini (Ehrich Weiss. Hungarian-born American magician and escape artist, 1874–1926). Houdini is probably the best-known name in magic, both past and present. Some of Houdini's well-known escapes were the Milk Can Escape, the Chinese Water Torture Cell Escape, and of course the Upside-Down Straitjacket Escape. Houdini also appeared in several films. It is also interesting to note that Houdini was fascinated with flying and made his first flight in Hamburg, Germany. When he toured Australia, he brought his airplane with him and had the distinction of being the first person to achieve controlled power flight in Australia. Houdini was also known for his efforts to debunk spiritualism in the 1920s.

Bill Hunter (American magician, b. 1923). Bill Hunter is best known as Bill "Magic 500" Hunter, as he has entertained at the world-famous Indianapolis 500 racetrack for over forty years. It is interesting to note that Hunter was introduced to magic in a recovery hospital in World War II by the world-famous middleweight boxer, Steve Belloise. Bill Hunter is one of the best at walkaround close-up magic.

Joshua Jay (American magician, b. 1981). Joshua Jay is one of the finest magicians in the world. He is also one of the best lecturers on magic. Joshua has performed and lectured around the world. He is probably best known for his innovative close-up magic. He has authored several books on the subject of magic. I would highly recommend any of Joshua's books, DVDs, or products to anyone interested in magic. I first met Joshua at one of his lectures. I like the way he explains techniques in a way that anyone can understand easily. One of the best quotes of Joshua's that I live by is: "If a simple, easy to do technique or method can achieve the same effect as a complicated move or method, then use it. Don't be afraid to improvise and try new methods." As a blind magician, I have used this advice many times. Joshua is a remarkable person who is more than willing to help any person who is interested in magic. He is not only a friend but also is one of the friendliest people you will ever meet.

Jonathan Kamm (American magician, b. 1964). Jonathan Kamm is an expert at close-up magic who specializes in close-up restaurant magic. He is known for his brilliant, innovative card magic. He has produced many effects on the Internet, and it is interesting to know that he has the most-viewed and highest rated Ambitious Card routine on the Internet. In fact, Wikipedia (the online encyclopedia) used Jonathan's video as an example of the Ambitious Card routine. Jonathan is the creator of many unique card magic effects. Jonathan has been the house magician at the famous Walter Payton's Roundhouse in Aurora, Illinois, for thirteen years and has been a professional magician for over twenty-five years. I would highly recommend that you check out his videos on the Internet.

Harry Kellar (Heinrich Kellar, American magician and illusionist, 1849–1922). Harry Kellar was one of the greatest magicians in history. He would travel to many different countries with his large stage show during the late 1800s and early 1900s. He was often referred to as the "Dean of American Magicians.

Nate Leipzig (Nathan Leipziger, Swedish-born American magician, 1873–1939). Nate Leipzig was sometimes referred to as the magician's magician. He was famous for his close-up magic that he performed on stage. He would have a committee of people come up on stage to watch his performance, and the audience would enjoy the show through the reaction of the committee. It is believed that Leipzig developed many of the sleight-of-hand techniques that are still used today by close-up magicians.

Jeff McBride (American magician, b. 1958). Jeff McBride is known for his expertise with card manipulation and his outstanding stage magic that combines magic with Japanese Kabuki theater. Jeff is also well known as a teacher of magic and has been an inspiration to many magicians, helping them to develop world-class routines.

Norm Nielsen (American magician, b. 1934). Norm Nielsen is one of the world's best magicians. He is probably best known for his musical magic act and the Floating Violin, which is one of the most beautiful routines in magic. Norm Nielsen is also one of the finest manufacturers of high-quality magic. At one time, I owned a Nielsen Vanishing Dove Cage, and I must say the craftsmanship is fantastic. I am honored to be able to call Mr. Nielsen a friend. He is one of the nicest persons I have ever met.

Penn & Teller (Penn Frasser Jillette, b. 1955, and Raymond Joseph Teller, b. 1948). Penn & Teller are known for their comedy magic and have performed together for over thirty years. They have appeared in many TV specials, as well as many theatrical films. They also have performed for sold-out audiences in Las Vegas. Penn & Teller are the authors of several books about magic.

Zack Percell (American magician, b. 1975). Zack Percell performs all types of magic for all types of audiences. Whether it is a school show for kids, or adults at a nightclub, Zack provides great magical entertainment. What is interesting is that one of Zack's first experiences with magic was when the Amazing Haundini performed at his elementary school. Another student, a fourth grader, who saw the Amazing Haundini perform that day, was another future magician named Todd Ripplinger. Eventually, Todd and Zack would combine their magical talents and be known as the Magical Adventures of TnZ. They had a fantastic show and performed at many events in the United States and would also perform in Japan. Tragically, Todd Ripplinger (1978–2003) drowned while surfing in Maui. Like Zack, Todd was not only a talented magician, but he also was one of the nicest people you could ever meet. He will be missed not only by his friends and family but by the entire magic fraternity as well. Zack eventually put a solo act together. He kept the name TnZ in honor of Todd. Zack can perform any venue at a professional level. I especially like his mentalism routines. He performs a Spirit Slate routine that fools many magicians.

Channing Pollock (American magician and film actor, 1926–2006). Without a doubt, Channing Pollock was one of magic's most charismatic performers. He was best known for his dove routine. It is interesting to note that Channing Pollock performed for many famous people, such as President Eisenhower, Queen Elizabeth II, and at the wedding of Prince Rainier and Grace Kelly. As an actor, Channing Pollock appeared in many theatrical films and in a number of television series.

James Randi (Randall James Hamilton Zwinge, Canadian-born American magician, escape artist, and scientific skeptic, b. 1928). James Randi is probably better known as the Amazing Randi. He is famous as a scientific skeptic who challenges those who make claims of paranormal or supernatural abilities. He is the founder of the James Randi Educational Foundation. In 1964, Randi put up a thousand dollars of his own money to anyone who could provide proof of the paranormal or of supernatural powers. Today, the foundation is well known for its million-dollar challenge. This is a prize of one million dollars to anyone who can demonstrate evidence of paranormal or supernatural powers under test conditions. So far, no one has received the money. The Amazing Randi has appeared on several TV shows, both as a magician and a skeptic.

Richiardi (Aldo Izquierdo Coloso, Peruvian magician, 1923–1965). Richiardi came from a family of magicians. Richiardi was best known for his gory illusions. For example, he would perform the classic illusion Sawing a Lady in Half in a bizarre performance. He would use fake blood and make it appear as though he was actually sawing his assistant in half! In a June 8, 2007, appearance on the *Late Late Show with Craig Ferguson,* Criss Angel said that Richiardi was one of his biggest influences.

Shimada (Haruo Shimada, Japanese-born American magician, b. 1940). Shimada is one of the world's finest magicians and is legendary for his dove magic. Shimada was the first Japanese entertainer to star in a Las Vegas show for an extended multiyear contract. I met Shimada at a magicians convention. He is not only a great magician, but he also is one of the friendliest and nicest people in magic.

Siegfried & Roy (Martin Siegfried Fischbacher, b. 1939, and Roy Horn, b. 1944, German-born American magicians and illusionists). Siegfried & Roy are probably the best-known magicians in the world. Their show was one of the biggest draws in Las Vegas. They have received about every award and honor in magic. In 1999 Siegfried & Roy received a star on the famous Hollywood Walk of Fame. Unfortunately, during a show in 2003, Roy was bitten by his beloved tiger, Montecore and was critically injured. Roy has been in rehabilitation for over five years. Siegfried & Roy performed their last show on March 1, 2009.

I met Siegfried & Roy in the early 1980s. I was attending a magicians convention, and part of the convention was a get-together at Siegfried & Roy's mansion. It is beautiful. I got to talk to Siegfried & Roy while having our picture taken. Siegfried asked me what kind of magic I did, and Roy asked me if I ever used animals in my magic show. Siegfried & Roy are great people, both on stage and off. While they are among the greatest magicians in the world, their greatness is being the nice and friendly people they are.

Slydini (Quintino Marucci Foggia, Italian-born American magician, 1900–1991). Slydini was one of the best magicians of all time. His magic was much more than a performance of excellent technique. It was a form of art. Slydini was a master of close-up magic, and his mastery was in his presentation. His close-up magic was more than a collection of tricks. It was a way to involve the audience as part of the magic. He used magic much like a painter applies paint to a canvas to produce a beautiful picture. I met Slydini in Las Vegas and was fortunate to be able to talk with him for a while. He showed me how to tie a false knot in a silk. He was so nice. Slydini's mastery of technique was secondary to his mastery with people.

Chung Ling Soo (William Ellsworth Robinson, American magician, 1868–1918). Chung Ling Soo was probably made famous by his dying while performing his Bullet Catching routine. The gimmicked gun was supposed to drop the bullet into a chamber. Chung Ling Soo performed his well-known routine on March 23, 1918, in a London theater. However, the gun was not cleaned properly, and the bullet was loaded into the barrel. Chung Ling Soo was killed when the bullet struck him in the chest. It is interesting to note that Chung Ling Soo never spoke English in public. He took his act as a Chinese magician very seriously and would use an interpreter to speak with news reporters.

The Great Tomsoni (Johnny Thompson, American magician). The Great Tomsoni is one of the best magicians in the world. He performs with his lovely wife, Pam. His comedy magic is really funny and entertaining. Johnny is also a great teacher of magic and is a mentor to many magicians, including Lance Burton, Penn & Teller, and Criss Angel. I was fortunate to be able to talk to Johnny and Pam at the last magicians convention I attended. They are both so nice and friendly. They have a way of making everyone who talks to them feel special.

Howard Thurston (American magician, 1869–1936). Howard Thurston was one of the best-known magicians of all time. He traveled around the country doing large stage shows. His show was so large that it required eight train cars to carry his stage equipment. He was known as the King of Cards and was one of the first magicians to make back-palming a part of his routine.

Dai Vernon (David Frederick Wingfield Verner, Canadian magician, 1894–1992). Dai Vernon was a master at sleight of hand and close-up magic. He was also a mentor to many famous magicians. He was called the Professor because he had such an extensive knowledge about magic. I met Dai Vernon at the first magicians convention I attended in the early 1980s. He was interested that I was a blind magician and asked me a few questions about how I performed certain tricks. I told him some of the methods I used. I told him there were certain things I couldn't do because I can't see but that I have found methods to overcome my limitations. Dai Vernon then gave me this advice: "While it certainly is important to have great technique, the

243

real magic is in the presentation." It has been advice that I have incorporated into any magic routine that I do.

Mark Wilson (James Mark Wilson, American magician, b. 1929). Mark Wilson is credited with being the first television magician. In October 1960, Wilson created the magic show called *The Magic Land of Allakazam*. I remember watching this show on Saturday mornings. Later, Wilson created other TV magic shows, such as *The Funny Face Magic Show*, and in 1971 he created *Magic Circus*. Also in 1971, Wilson published *Mark Wilson's Complete Course in Magic*, which is one of the best resources to learn magic.

Mike "Magic Mike" Winters (American magician, b. 1957). Mike Winters is a full time professional magician who is multitalented in the art of magic. He performs close-up and stage magic at many events around the country. He also has a fantastic stage hypnosis routine. I like the way Mike interjects humor into his magic. He connects with the audience in a very entertaining way. Like many magicians, Magic Mike continually studies the art of magic. He is always quick to help a fellow magician. I am fortunate to have Mike as a friend, and the magic fraternity is fortunate to have him as such an outstanding example of what it is to be a magician.

Magic Organizations

Once you become involved in magic, you might want to consider joining a magic organization. These organizations are an excellent resource for learning more about magic.

International Brotherhood of Magicians (IBM)
13 Point West Blvd.
St. Charles, MO 63301-4431
Phone: (636) 724-2400

International Magicians Society (IMS)
581 Ellison Ave.
Westbury, NY 11590
Phone: (516) 333-2377

Society of American Magicians (SAM)
National Administrator
P.O. Box 510260
St. Louis, MO 63151

Suggested Reading

There are many fine books on the subject of magic. There are books on the history of magic, the performance of magic, and famous magicians. One of the best ways to learn magic is to start with a book on beginning magic. There are several how-to-do magic books at your local library.

The following is a list of the magic books I have in my personal library. I recommend them, and I am sure you will find them very informative and enjoyable to read.

Mark Wilson's Complete Course in Magic by Mark Wilson. Running Press Book Publishers, 1991.
This is one of my favorite magic books. It is a complete course on magic and covers many different subjects. It is well illustrated, and the explanations are clear and easy to understand.

The Tarbell Course in Magic by Harlan E. Tarbell. Volumes One to Eight. D. Robbins & Co., Inc., 1971.
This is an actual course on magic. It has been revised and updated over the years. It covers all areas of magic. This is one of the first sets of books I bought when I was learning to do magic. There are eight volumes in the set. Each volume has lessons. For example, Volume One has lessons 1 to 19. Volume Two has lessons 20 to 33, and so on. I still use it as a reference on performing certain effects. I highly recommend the Tarbell Course to anyone who is getting started in magic.

The Greater Magic Library by John Northern Hilliard. Complete in Five Volumes. A.S. Barnes and Company, 1956.
This is a large book and covers many different areas of magic. It covers mostly card magic but also includes others areas, like coins, silks, sponge balls, etc. It is very comprehensive, and many magicians use this book as a reference.

Scarne on Card Tricks by John Scarne. Random House Value Publishing, 1988.
This book explains over 150 card tricks. It is written very well and is easy to understand. This book is considered by many magicians to be a classic work on card magic.

The Illustrated History of Magic by Milbourne Christopher. Crowell, 1973.
This book covers the history of magic and many famous magicians. It is a pleasure to read and very informative on the history of magic.

Encyclopedia of Card Tricks (Cards, Coins, and Other Magic) by Jean Hugard. Dover Publications, 1974.

This book is very comprehensive and covers mostly card tricks. It also covers many others subjects as well. It is a very good reference book for those interested in card magic.

Modern Coin Magic by J. B. Bobo. Dover, 1982.
This is a classic work on coin magic. It covers about everything you would want to know about coin magic.

The World's Greatest Magic by Hyla Clark. Random House Value Publishing, 1988.
This is a coffee-table–type of book with many nice photographs of famous magicians. This is one of my favorite magic books. I took this book to many of the magicians conventions I have attended and got it autographed by many of the magicians who are featured in the book.

The Anthology of Card Magic by Gordon Miller. Abbott's, 1989.
This is a very comprehensive book about all types of card magic. Abbott's Magic has been putting card tricks in their catalogs for many years. There have been hundreds of great card tricks published in the catalog. This book is an anthology of those card tricks. There are over three hundred tricks in this book!

Stars of Magic by George Starke. Meir Yedid Magic, 2008.
I personally feel this is one of the best books on magic. Originally, *Stars of Magic* was published as a series. It featured some of the legends in magic, like Dai Vernon, Tony Slydini, John Scarne, Nate Leipzig, Max Malini, Emil Jarrow, and more. These lessons are for the more advanced magician and teach some of the classic close-up effects, such as Triumph and Spellbound. These are actually taught by the Professor himself, the legendary Dai Vernon. The book is well illustrated with many photographs.

Magic: The Complete Course in Becoming a Magician by Joshua Jay. Workman Publishing Company, 2008.This course is available in a book or DVD. This is a great book for those wanting to learn magic.

Magic Terminology

Apparatus. The props and equipment used in a magic show.

Assistant. A person who helps the magician during his act.

Back-palming. To conceal a card or other object behind the hand.

Bottom dealing. To deal a card from the bottom of the deck.

Break. To slightly hold open a portion of the deck of cards.

Change. To transform one object for another.

Clean. Finishing a routine without a trace of how the magic was done.

Close-up magic. A magic routine performed with cards, coins, sponges, etc., within close proximity to the audience.

Color change. To transform the color of an object into a different color.

Confederate. A spectator who is working with the magician.

Conjurer. Another name for a magician.

Cut. To separate one portion of a deck of cards.

Dealing seconds. To deal the second card from the top of a deck of cards.

Dealing thirds. To deal the third card from the top of a deck of cards.

Disappearance. To make an object vanish.

Effect. Another term for magic trick.

False cut. To make it appear as though a cut is made when in reality the deck has not been cut.

Fan. To evenly spread out a deck of cards.

Finger palm. To secretly retain an object within the folds of the fingers.

Flashing. To expose an object that is supposed to be hidden.

Flash paper. Specially treated paper that bursts into flames when it comes in contact with a match or other fire.

Flourish. To display an object or a deck of cards in an artistic presentation.

Force. To make a spectator select a chosen card that he thinks is a free choice.

Gaffed. A secretly prepared card, coin, or other object that is made to perform a magic effect.

Gimmick. Another term for gaffed.

Glimpse. To secretly look at a card during a card routine.

Holdout. A device that enables a performer to produce, vanish, or change a deck of cards.

Illusion. A large stage prop used in the performance of magic.

Jog. To offset one portion of cards from another.

Legerdemain. Another term for magic, usually in regard to sleight of hand.

Levitation. To make an object or person rise in a magical way.

Load. An object secretly hidden on the magician.

Marked deck. A specially prepared deck of cards that makes it easy for the magician to know what the individual cards are.

Mentalism. Magic of the mind, including mind reading and psychic effects. The magician appears to have extra-sensory perception (ESP) and can predict future events.

Misdirection. Directing the attention of the audience away from the action that the magician doesn't want them to see.

Move. A sleight of hand technique or action.

Packet trick. A card trick done with a few cards and, in many cases, specially prepared cards.

Palm or palming. To secretly retain an object in the palm of the hand.

Pass. A sleight-of-hand technique.

Patter. The words a magician uses during a routine.

Peg. To physically mark a card.

Penetration. To make one solid object pass through another.

Prestidigitation. Another term for magic, specifically sleight of hand.

Produce or production. To make an object appear from an empty apparatus or from thin air.

Reset. An effect that is ready to be performed immediately after doing the effect.

Ribbon Spread. To spread out a deck of cards evenly.

Riffle. The sound and motion of pushing down with the thumb on the corners on a deck of cards.

Routine. A segment of a magic performance or a pattern of movements that makes a complete magic act.

Self-working trick. A trick that takes no skill or difficult technique to perform.

Shell. A hollowed-out object that can conceal another object.

Shiner. A shiny mirror object used to glimpse a card.

Short card. A card that is cut shorter than other cards, used for locating a card in the deck.

Shuffle. To mix up a deck of cards.

Silk. A thin, colorful, and compressible cloth. Silks come in many different colors and sizes.

Sleight of hand. Techniques of magic with cards.

Stacked deck. A deck that has been prearranged in a certain order.

Steal. To secretly take possession of an object without the audience's knowledge.

Street magic. Magic that is performed in open areas, such as street corners, sidewalks, and boulevards.

Stripper deck. A gimmicked deck that allows the easy location of a card or groups of cards.

Svengali deck. A gimmicked deck that can be used for many different card tricks, including turning a full deck into all the same card.

Switch. To substitute one object for another.

Table-hopping. Performing magic from one table to another, as in restaurants or bars.

Talk. The accidental clicking of one object striking another during a magic routine.

Transposition. To make one object change place or appear as another object.

Two-sided card. A gimmicked card that has two faces or two backs.

Vanish. To make an object disappear.

Volunteer. A person selected to help the magician in a magic routine.

Bibliography and Sources

Allen, Jon. *Simple Magic Tricks.* Octopus Publishing Group, 2004.

Bobo, J. B. *Modern Coin Magic.* Dover Publications, 1982.

Dawes, Edwin and Setterington, Arthur. *The Encyclopedia of Magic.* Gallery Books, 1988.

Downs, Thomas Nelson. *Modern Coin Manipulation.* T. Nelson Downs Magical Co., 1900.

Eldin, Peter. *The Most Excellent Book of How to Do Card Tricks.* Aladdin Books, 1996.

Erdnase, S. W. *The Expert at the Card Table: The Classic Treatise on Card Manipulation.* Dover Publications, 1995.

Evans, Cheryl and Keable-Elliott, Ian. *Complete Book of Magic.* Usborne Publishing, 1989.

Fulves, Karl. *Self-Working Close-Up Card Magic: 56 Foolproof Tricks.* Dover Publications, 1995.

Fulves, Karl. *Self-Working Coin Magic: 92 Foolproof Tricks.* Dover Publications, 1990.

Ganson, Lewis. *Routine Manipulation Vol. 1 & 2.* Louis Tannen. 1976.

Heddle, Rebecca and Keable, Ian. *Book of Magic Tricks.* Usborne Publishing, 1991.

Marlo, Ed. *The Cardician.* Magic, Inc., 1973.
Marlo, Ed. *Let's See the Deck.* L. L. Ireland, 1942.
Marlo, Ed. *Revolutionary Card Technique.* Magic, 2003.

Mentzer, Jerry. *Counts Cuts Moves and Subtlety ... a Book of Basic Card Technique.* Jerry Mentzer, 1980.

Miller, Gordon. *Abbott's: The Anthology of Card Magic.* Abbott's, 1989.

Smith, Bruce. *Great Coin Tricks.* Sterling Publishing Company, 1995.

Tarr, Bill. *101 Easy-to-Do Magic Tricks.* Dover Publications, 1992.
Tarr, Bill. *Now You See It, Now You Don't!: Lessons in Sleight of Hand.* Vintage Books, 1976.

Wade, John. *Teach Yourself Magic Tricks.* NTC Publishing Group, 1992.

Willmarth, Philip. *The Magic of Matt Schulien.* Media Books, 1959.

Wilson, Mark. *Mark Wilson's Complete Course in Magic.* Courage Books, 1991.

References and Acknowledgements for Effects and Methods

I have tried to list the creator or inventor of the effects used in this book. I have researched many sources to try to provide the proper credit for anything I might have used in the book. Many card magic effects are found by different names by different people. Certain card tricks, such as the Fingerprint Detection, Pulse Detection, Four Ace Assembly, and the Impossible Location trick, are found in several different sources by different authors.

I am not the creator or inventor of any magic used in this book. These effects and principles (such as the Key Card Principle) have been around for many years. Many magicians have added variations or have made the trick easier to do by some different method. As a blind magician, I have had to adapt the magic in this book so that I could perform it without the use of sight. Usually this means that I must know beforehand the location of certain cards or must set up the deck before a performance. At other times, I will openly ask a spectator to name a card for me.

I would like to thank any magician, past and present, who has created or invented a magic trick. In doing so, he has indeed brought magic into the lives of someone else. And that, my friends, is the best magic in the world.

The Coin Control Card. This is found in *Magic of Matt Schulien* by Philip Willmarth. Media Books, 1959.

Card Magic

1. You Do It! I was originally taught this trick when I first started taking card magic classes. A version of this trick can be found in *Easy Card Magic* by Bob Longe. Sterling Publications, 1995. It's All Yours, p. 114.

2. No-Problem Card Location. I was originally taught this trick when I was in the Veterans Hospital for Blind Rehabilitation. A version of this trick is found in *Self-Working Card Tricks: 72 Foolproof Card Miracles for the Amateur Magician* by Karl Fulves. Dover Publications, 1976. No-Clue Discovery, p. 1.

3. Five Times Five Equals Magic. I was originally taught this trick when I first started taking magic classes at a local magic shop. A version of this trick is found in *Card Magic: 117 Easy-to-Perform Tricks with an Ordinary Deck* by Bill Okal. Paragon-Reiss, 1982. The Magic of 7, p. 16.

4. Reverse Reveal-ation. I was originally taught this trick in card magic classes when I first became interested in doing magic. A version of this trick can be found in *Easy Card Magic* by Rob Roy. Robbins & Co., 1972. The Turned-Up Bottom, p. 21.

5. Four Sisters Reunion. This is one of the first tricks I learned as a magician. As a blind magician, all I need to know is that I have the correct cards on top and bottom. I then put the other two Queens where I know they are located. A version of this trick is found on *Amazing Magic Tricks with Cards* by Fun Incorporated. Royal Magic, 2002. The Nun trick shown by Dave Hudspath.

6. I Can Hear It Now. This is one of the first tricks I learned. A version of this trick is found on *Easy to Learn Magic Series. Vol. 2.* Distron Video Group, 2005. Card Magic by Tony Hassini.

7. The Lie Detector Deck. This is one of the first tricks I learned when I began magic classes. As a blind magician, all I needed to know was what the Key Card was before I performed the trick. This is a classic of card magic and is found in many card magic books. A version of this trick is found in *Magic with Cards: 113 Easy-to-Perform Miracles with an Ordinary Deck of Cards* by Frank Garcia and George Schindler. Barnes & Noble, 1975. Tell the Truth, p. 11.

8, Telepathy Times Two. A version of this trick is found in *200 Magic Tricks Anyone Can Do* by Harry Blackstone. Citadel Press Books, which are published by Kensington Publications, 1983. Two Numbers, p. 99.

9. Side by Side. A version of this trick is found in *Easy Card Magic* by Bob Longe. Sterling Publications, 1992. Same Old, Same Old, p. 82. Attributed to the great card man Ed Marlo.

10. Jacks or Better. A version of this trick is found in *My Best Self-Working Card Tricks* by Karl Fulves. Dover Publications, 2001. Eleven and One, p. 19.

11. High Voltage. A version of this trick is found in *Card Magic: 117 Easy-to-Perform Tricks with an Ordinary Deck* by Bill Okal. Paragon-Reiss, 1982. The Fingerprint Test, p. 17.

12. The Royal Treatment. A version of this trick is found in *Easy Card Magic* by Rob Roy. Robbins & Co., 1972. The Royal Blush, p. 17.

13. Pushed-Out Prediction. A version of this trick is found on the *Amazing Magic Tricks with Cards* DVD by Fun Incorporated, Royal Magic, 2002. Second trick by Dave Hudspath.

14. Double-Decker Prediction. A version of this trick is found in *Simple Magic Tricks: Easy-to-Learn Magic Tricks with Everyday Objects* by Jon Allen. Octopus Publishing Group Ltd., 2004. Always Get It Right, p. 8.

15. X Marks the Spot. A version of this trick is found in *Mark Wilson's Course on Magic* by Mark Wilson. Running Press Books, 1981. Original edition published by Ottenheimer Publications for Courage Books. The Double X Mystery, p. 38.

16. Yours and Mine. A version of this trick is found in *101 Easy-to-Do Magic Tricks* by Bill Tarr. Vintage Books, 1977. Double Reverse, p. 94. Attributed originally to Nate Leipzig.

17. Red-Black Revelation. A version of this trick is found in *My Best Self-Working Card Tricks* by Karl Fulves. Dover Publications, 2001. Color of Thought, p. 37.

18. Cards of a Feather. A version of this trick is found in *Card Magic: 117 Easy-to-Perform Tricks with an Ordinary Deck* by Bill Okal. Paragon-Reiss, 1982. Cards of Affinity, p. 27.

19. Six in the Mix. A version of this trick is found in *Easy Card Magic* by Rob Roy. Robbins & Co., 1972. Severn Keys, p. 6.

20. The Lady with X-ray Vision. A version of this trick is found in *Easy-to-Do Card Tricks for Children* by Karl Fulves. Dover Publications, 1989. Twenty Twenty, p. 23.

21. Magic Almanac. A version of this trick is found in *Magic with Cards: 113 Easy-to-Perform Miracles with an Ordinary Deck of Cards* by Frank Garcia and George Schindler. Barnes & Noble, 1975. Quick Year, p. 19.

22. Face Up & Face Down. A version of this trick is found in *200 Magic Tricks Anyone Can Do* by Harry Blackstone. Citadel Press Books, which are published by Kensington Publications, 1983. Reversing Cards, p. 107.

23. The Outta Sight Prediction Trick. A version of this trick is found in *Simple Magic Tricks: Easy-to-Learn Magic Tricks with Everyday Objects* by Jon Allen. Octopus Publishing Group Ltd., 2004. The Undercover Card, p. 16.

24. Jack-in-the-Box. A version of this trick is found on the website *ehow.com.* Published by ehow.com, 2009. Card Predictions, Magic Trick Technique by Wayne Phelps for expert village. com.

25. The *Amazing* Spectator. A version of this trick is found in *101 Easy-to-Do Magic Tricks* by Bill Tarr. Vintage Books, 1977. You're the magician, p. 90.

26. The Magic of Three. I was first taught this trick when I began taking card magic classes. It is one of the first card tricks I learned. A version of this trick is found in *Easy Card Magic* by Bob Longe. Sterling Publications, 1995. And Four to Go, p. 58.

27. Cardiac Card. I was taught this trick when I first began card magic classes. I use a pegged card so that I can feel the Key Card. I then know the spectator's chosen card is next to it. A version of this trick is found on *Amazing Tricks with Cards* DVD by Fun Incorporated. Royal Magic, 2002. Pulse card by Dave Hudspath.

28. Doc Does It Again. A version of this trick is found in *Self-Working Close-Up Card Magic: 56 Foolproof Tricks* by Karl Fulves. Dover Publications, 1995. Beat A Cheat, p. 48. Effect originally devised by Stewart James.

29. The Magical Happy Birthday Trick. A version of this trick can be found in *200 Magic Tricks Anyone Can Do* by Harry Blackstone. Citadel Press Books, which are published by Kensington Publications, 1983. Yankee Doodle, p. 140.

30. Ace through the Deck. A version of this trick is found in *Easy Card Magic* by Rob Roy. Robbins & Co. 1972. Flying Aces, p. 10.

31. A Roll of the Dice. I was taught this trick when I first began taking card magic classes. One of the best explanations of the trick was done by Criss Angel on his TV show *Mindfreak*. Arts and Entertainment Network (A&E), 2009.

Money Magic

1. Flash Cash. This trick was contributed by Joshua Jay. It is in his excellent course on magic titled *MAGIC: The Complete Course.* Workman Publishing, 2008. This is one of the finest magic courses available. It comes with a DVD. I would highly recommend this book to anyone interested in magic. Bank Roll, p. 202. Joshua Jay gives credit on the technique used is his version to Max Maven. The technique is known as the Rhythm Switch and was first published in *Jinx* in 1967. I have adapted the switch to make it easier for me to do. I simply put the paper roll and real roll in the same pocket and switch them when I pull out the rubber band.

2. Turnover Coin Vanish. This is one of the first coin tricks I learned when I began magic classes. A version of this trick is found in *Magic Library Great Coin Tricks* by Bruce Smith. Sterling Publications, 2000. First published in Great Britain under the title *Coin and Banknote Tricks* in 1995 by Archurus Publishing Ltd. Jumping Coins, p. 5.

3. A Hole in One. I was taught how to do this trick when I was in the Veterans Hospital for Blind Rehabilitation. A version of this trick is found in *Self-Working Table Magic: 97 Foolproof Tricks with Ordinary Objects* by Karl Fulves. Dover Publications, 1981. Hole in the Pocket, p. 7.

4. The Hypnotized Half. A version of this trick is found on the DVD *Amazing Magic Tricks with Money* by Fun Incorporated. Royal Magic, 2002. Half-dollar trick as demonstrated by Dave Hudspath.

5. The Magic Circle of Coins. A version of this trick is found in *Simple Magic Tricks: Easy-to-Learn Magic Tricks with Everyday Objects* by Jon Allen. Octopus Publishing Group Ltd., 2004. Alphabetical Assistance, p. 78.

6. Into Thin Air! A version of this trick is found In *101 Easy-to-Do Magic Tricks* by Bill Tarr. Vintage Books, 1977. An Easy Coin Vanish, p. 192.

7. Top Five. This is one of the first money tricks I learned. I have probably done this trick over a thousand times, as it can be done at any time using borrowed money. A version of this trick is found in *Self-Working Coin Magic: 92 Foolproof Tricks* by Karl Fulves. Dover Publications, 1989. Five Riser, p. 4.

8. Silver Express. A version of this trick can be found in *Mark Wilson's Complete Course in Magic* by Mark Wilson. Running Press Books, 1981. Original edition published by Ottenheimer Publications for Courage Books. The Coin Fold, p. 177.

9. Compound Interest. A version of this trick is found in *Magic Library Great Coin Tricks* by Bruce Smith. Sterling Publications, 2000. First published in Great Britain under the title *Coin and Banknote Tricks* in 1995 by Archurus Publishing Ltd. Multiply Your Money, p. 29.

A similar version that uses a nickel and two half-dollars is found in *Mark Wilson's Complete Course in Magic* by Mark Wilson. Running Press Books, 1981. Magically Multiply Your Money, p. 181.

10. It's in the Mail! A version of this trick is found in *Self-Working Table Magic: 97 Foolproof Tricks with Ordinary Objects* by Karl Fulves. Dover Publications, 1981. Sealed Silver, p. 8.

11. Counterfeit Connection. A version of this trick is found on the DVD *Amazing Magic Tricks with Money* by Fun Incorporated. Royal Magic, 2002. Good with Money as demonstrated by David Hudspath.

12. A Visit to the Mint. A version of this trick is found in *Self-Working Coin Magic: 92 Foolproof Tricks* by Karl Fulves. Dover Publications, 1989. Money Makes Money, p. 14. The move to shift the coin from one side to the other is credited to Clayton Rosencrance.

13. Magical Moneymaker. This trick is found in several different magic books and videos. A version of this trick is found in *Greater Magic Library Great Coin Tricks* by Bruce Smith. First published in Great Britain under the title *Coin and Banknote Tricks* in 1995 by Archurus Publishing Ltd. Continuous Coins, p. 33.

14. In the Money! A version of this trick is found on the DVD *Amazing Magic Tricks with Money* by Fun Incorporated. Royal Magic, 2002. Pencil and dollar trick as demonstrated by David Hudspath. There is also a nice version of this in *Greater Magic Library Great Coin Tricks* by Bruce Smith. First published in Great Britain under the title *Coin and Banknote Tricks* in 1995 by Archurus Publishing Ltd. Pencil through Note, p. 123.

15. Smooth Move. A version of this trick is found in *Simple Magic Tricks: Easy-to-Learn Magic Tricks with Everyday Objects* by Jon Allen. Octopus Publishing Group Ltd., 2004. Where on Earth …?, p. 82.

16. Gone—but Not for Long! A version of this trick is found in *Mark Wilson's Complete Course in Magic* by Mark Wilson. Running Press Books, 1981. Original edition published by Ottenheimer Publications for Courage Books. Coin-a-Go-Go, p. 197.

17. Right on the Money! A version of this trick is found on the DVD *Amazing Magic Tricks with Money* by Fun Incorporated. Royal Magic, 2002. Coin prediction as demonstrated by Davie Hudspath.

18. Bread Money. A version of this trick is found in *Simple Magic Tricks: Easy-to-Learn Magic Tricks with Everyday Objects* by Jon Allen. Octopus Publishing Group Ltd., 2004. Sandwich Secrets, p. 83. There is also a nice version of this trick in *Greater Magic Library Great Coin Tricks* by Bruce Smith. First published in Great Britain under the title *Coin and Banknote Tricks* in 1995 by Archurus Publishing Ltd. Dough!, p. 112.

19. Coin through the Table. There are many versions of this trick found in books and videos on the subject of coin magic. A version of this trick is found in *Self-Working Coin Magic: 92 Foolproof Tricks* by Karl Fulves. Dover Publications, 1989. Tunnel Move, p. 27. Credit is given to Slydini.

20. Magical Multi-Money Prediction. A version of this trick is found on the DVD *Amazing Magic Tricks with Money* by Fun Incorporated. Royal Magic, 2002. Several coins prediction as demonstrated by Davie Hudspath.

Mental Magic

1. The Nose Knows! A version of this trick is found in *Self-Working Mental Magic: 67 Foolproof Mind reading Tricks* by Karl Fulves. Dover Publications, 1979. Money Sense, p. 1. Credit is given to Stuart Robson.

2. It's in the Numbers! A version of this trick is found in *200 Magic Tricks Anyone Can Do* by Harry Blackstone. Citadel Press Books, which are published by Kensington Publications, 1983. Total Foretold, p. 197.

3. Mind Power Prediction. A version of this trick is found in *Simple Magic Tricks: Easy-to-Learn Magic Tricks with Everyday Objects* by Jon Allen. Octopus Publishing Group Ltd., 2004. Memorizing with a Difference, p. 90.

4. That's Impossible! Book Test. A version of this trick is found in *200 Magic Tricks Anyone Can Do* by Harry Blackstone. Citadel Press Books, which are published by Kensington Publications, 1983. Choose Your Word, p. 182.

5. That's Your Word. A version of this trick is found in *Mark Wilson's Complete Course in Magic* by Mark Wilson. Running Press Books, 1981. Original edition published by Ottenheimer Publications for Courage Books. Magazine Test, p. 322.

6. Amazing Mind Transposition. A version of this trick is found in *Self-Working Mental Magic: 67 Foolproof Mind reading Tricks* by Karl Fulves. Dover Publications, 1979. Think of a Word, p. 46.

7. Mind Over Matter. A version of this trick is found in *101 Easy-to-Do Magic Tricks* by Bill Tarr. Vintage Books, 1977. Table Divination, p. 113. Credit is given to Walter B. Gibson. Another easy to do version of this trick is found in *200 Magic Tricks Anyone Can Do* by Harry Blackstone. Citadel Press Books, which are published by Kensington Publications, 1983. Spell Your Choice, p. 197.

8. Magical Mystery Revelation. A version of this trick is found in *Simple Magic Tricks: Easy-to-Learn Magic Tricks with Everyday Objects* by Jon Allen. Octopus Publishing Group Ltd., 2004. Spot the Thief, p. 92.

9. Triple Telepathy. A version of this trick is found in *Card Magic: 117 Easy-to-Perform Tricks with an Ordinary Deck* by Bill Okal. Paragon-Reiss, 1982. Three of a Mind, p. 46.

10. The Mystery Key. A version of this trick is found in *Self-Working Mental Magic: 67 Foolproof Mind reading Tricks* by Karl Fulves. Dover Publications, 1979. Seven Keys, p. 67.

11. The Card Predictor Trick. A version of this trick is found on *Simple Magic Tricks: Easy-to-Learn Magic Tricks with Everyday Objects* by Jon Allen. Octopus Publishing Group Ltd., 2004. One Step Ahead of the Pack, p. 17.

12. The Mind reading Mentalist. A version of this trick is found in *Card Magic: 117 Easy-to-Perform Tricks with an Ordinary Deck* by Bill Okal. Paragon-Reiss, 1982. Predetermination, p. 48.

13. The Magic Number Book Test. A version of this trick is found on *Simple Magic Tricks: Easy-to-Learn Magic Tricks with Everyday Objects* by Jon Allen. Octopus Publishing Group Ltd., 2004. The Ultimate Math Trick, p. 96.

14. Super Mental Power Prediction. A version of this trick is found in *Magic with Cards: 113 Easy-to-Perform Miracles with an Ordinary Deck of Cards* by Frank Garcia and George Schindler. Barnes & Noble, 1975. Impromptu Prediction, p. 88.

15. Famous Forever. A version of this trick is found in *Mark Wilson's Complete Course in Magic* by Mark Wilson. Running Press Books, 1981. Original edition published by Ottenheimer Publications for Courage Books. The Curious Coincidence, p. 323.

Magic with Ordinary Objects

1. George Gets Clipped! A version of this trick is found in *101 Easy-to-Do Magic Tricks* by Bill Tarr. Vintage Books, 1977. Clipped, p. 198.

2. The Amazing Appearing Pencil. A version of this trick is found in *200 Magic Tricks Anyone Can Do* by Harry Blackstone. Citadel Press Books, which are published by Kensington Publications, 1983. Pencil from Matchbox, p. 162.

3. Let's Do the Twist! A version of this trick is found on *Simple Magic Tricks: Easy-to-Learn Magic Tricks with Everyday Objects* by Jon Allen. Octopus Publishing Group Ltd., 2004. Twist or Stick, p. 61.

4. The Impossible Pencil Penetration. A version of this trick is found in *Self-Working Table Magic: 97 Foolproof Tricks with Ordinary Objects* by Karl Fulves. Dover Publications. A Quick Getaway, p. 74. Credit is given to Ken Beale.

5. Super-Straw. A version of this trick is found in *200 Magic Tricks Anyone Can Do* by Harry Blackstone. Citadel Press Books, which are published by Kensington Publications, 1983. The Strong Straw, p. 18.

6. Pin Penetration. A version of this trick is found on *Simple Magic Tricks: Easy-to-Learn Magic Tricks with Everyday Objects* by Jon Allen. Octopus Publishing Group Ltd., 2004. Unlock the Pins Secret, p. 69.

7. Jumping Rubber Band. This trick is found in many beginning magic books. A version of this trick is found on *Simple Magic Tricks: Easy-to-Learn Magic Tricks with Everyday Objects* by Jon Allen. Octopus Publishing Group Ltd., 2004. Band on the Run, p. 64. Another good version is found in *Mark Wilson's Complete Course in Magic* by Mark Wilson. Running Press Books, 1981. Original edition published by Ottenheimer Publications for Courage Books. The Jumping Rubber Band, p. 295.

8. Cut and Restored String. I was taught this trick when I was in the Veterans Hospital for Blind Rehabilitation. A version of this trick is found on the DVD *Easy-to-Learn Magic Series: Beginner's Magic by* Tony Hassini. Distron Video Corp., and the International Magicians Society, 2005. Cut string through straw as demonstrated by Tony Hassini.

9. The Impossible Glass-on-Plate Effect. A version of this trick is found on *Simple Magic Tricks: Easy-to-Learn Magic Tricks with Everyday Objects* by Jon Allen. Octopus Publishing Group Ltd., 2004. A Balancing Act, p. 60.

10. Torn and Restored Napkin. A version of this trick is found in *Mark Wilson's Complete Course in Magic* by Mark Wilson. Running Press Books, 1981. Original edition published by Ottenheimer Publications for Courage Books. The Sucker Torn and Restored Napkin, p. 305.

Photo Credit

Cover photo: The Amazing Haundini and Dr. Jane Goodall, Gary and Rosie O'Donnell, Bill "Magic 500" Hunter, Gary and Renee photos courtesy of Kyler Photography.

The Amazing Haundini and "Gizmo the Magical Rabbit" courtesy of Collins Photography.

About the Author

As the Amazing Haundini, Gary Haun has entertained audiences, young and old, throughout the world. He has performed all types of magic, from close-up routines to large stage shows. He has performed magic on national TV and has been featured in a theatrical film. Gary is the first blind person ever to earn the Doctor of Magic diploma from the Magic Academy of the International Magicians Society.

The Amazing Haundini makes an appearance in the full length documentary film, Jane's Journey (2010) which is about his good friend, Dr. Jane Goodall. Jane Goodall is known throughout the world for her research of the chimpanzees in Africa as well as her concern for the environment. The film is directed by Lorenz Knauer who is not only a brilliant director but also uses his talents to bring attention to issues concerning the environment of the planet and the people who live in it. Angelina Jolie and Pierce Brosnan are also in the film.
Jane Goodall is a Messenger of Peace for the United Nations. Angelina Jolie is an Ambassador of Peace for the United Nations and is also known for her concern about environmental issues. Like Jane Goodall, Angelina Jolie has touched the lives of so many people in such a positive way.

Pierce Brosnan and his wife Keely Shaye Smith are well known for their charitable work and environmental activism.

While Angelina's husband, Brad Pitt is not in this film, I would personally like to thank him for his charitable work that has helped so many people.

These people do "true magic" which is in helping to make the world a better place to live.

In this book Gary reveals how magic has helped him overcome his limitations. As a blind magician, Gary explains what he has had to do to perform magic. He discusses the techniques and methods that have enabled him to become one of the world's finest blind magicians.

In *Diary of a Blind Magician*, Gary shares his passion for magic with you. He not only gives you some very interesting information about magic, but he actually teaches you how to perform some easy to do magic tricks.

Other Books by Gary Haun

VISION FROM THE HEART

In *Vision From the Heart*, Gary Haun shares his perspective on facing life's challenges. After losing his eyesight while in the Marine Corps, Gary did not let his limitations control his life. He hopes that by focusing on some of his experiences, others will push themselves in a positive direction. As Gary says, "When we accept the challenges in our lives, we can then attempt to overcome them."

This book contains Gary's personal philosophy. He has felt the snow on Mount Kilimanjaro and has been bumped around by Great White sharks. He tells what it is like from his perspective. In *Vision From the Heart*, Gary shares how he became a professional magician and a master instructor in Japanese Swordsmanship … and much more.

Introduction by Dr. Jane Goodall.
Available at Amazon.com, Barnes and Noble.com, and many other sources.

REFLECTIONS OF HELEN: AN ANALYSIS OF THE WORDS AND WISDOM OF HELEN KELLER: A SELF-HELP BOOK FOR ANYONE WHO IS FACING ADVERSITY

In *Reflections of Helen*, Gary explains how the words and wisdom of Helen Keller have helped him in his life. More importantly, he hopes this book will help *YOU* in your life. As Helen Keller overcame her limitations, Gary shows you how to overcome challenges in your life. In this book, Gary will help you find the magic that is within you.

Reflections of Helen will help you feel healthier and happier about your life. As Gary says, "We don't need sight to move in a positive direction. We need insight. The key to unlock the door to your future is inside you." This book can be a key to that door.